P9-CCO-670

Praise for StoryCorps titles

"A testimony to the power of narrative and vision . . . [*Ties That Bind*] is appealingly down-to-earth and, ultimately, moving."
—*Publishers Weekly*

"[*Ties That Bind*] is sweet and sad, heartwarming and watery-eye inducing. It's the kind of book that gives you the urge to call up someone important in your life, just to say hi."
—Associated Press

"As good as we humans are at division, we're better still at connection. *Ties That Bind* shows this again and again."
—Frank Bruni, *The New York Times*

"*All There Is* is a Valentine's Day gift more meaningful than any box of chocolates."
—*Entertainment Weekly*

"[A] collection of gems."
—*The Boston Globe*

"Heart-poundingly good . . . There's just one word for the book: lovely."
—*The Huffington Post*

"Bursts with stories that are unvarnished, sad, funny, wise, and, most of all, very real."
—*Chicago Tribune* (Editor's Choice)

"This latest compilation of StoryCorps vignettes will resonate with readers from varied backgrounds and different generations, spurring their own, perhaps log-buried, memories."
—*Booklist*

"[The stories in *Listening Is an Act of Love*] form shimmering threads in the American tapestry. . . . Read a few and you'll want to grab a loved one and share your own story."

—*People* (four star review)

"A page-turner . . . The StoryCorps stories feel both epic and intimate."

—*Culture + Travel*

"*Listening Is an Act of Love* is as heartwarming as a holiday pumpkin pie and every bit as homey. . . . What emerges in these compelling pages is hard-won wisdom and boundless humanity."

—John Marshall, *Seattle Post-Intelligencer*

"A veritable Noah's Ark of national character . . . These stories are extraordinary."

—*More*

"The stories are vivid and riveting. . . . A history of America as it is now."

—*The Star-Ledger* (Newark)

"[*Listening Is an Act of Love*] offers real insights into twentieth-century American life."

—Rose Jacobs, *Financial Times*

"Isay's ambition is nothing less than the largest oral history project in American history."

—Patrick Beach, *Austin American-Statesman*

PENGUIN BOOKS

TIES THAT BIND

Dave Isay is the founder of StoryCorps and the recipient of numerous broadcasting honors, including six Peabody awards and a MacArthur "Genius" Fellowship.

He is the author/editor of numerous books that grew out of his public radio documentary work, including three StoryCorps books: *Listening Is an Act of Love* (2007), *Mom: A Celebration of Mothers from StoryCorps* (2010), and *All There Is: Love Stories from StoryCorps* (2012)—all *New York Times* bestsellers. Isay is also an executive producer of StoryCorps Animated Shorts, as seen on the PBS documentary series *POV.*

TIES
THAT BIND

Stories of Love and Gratitude
from the First Ten Years
of StoryCorps

DAVE ISAY

WITH LIZZIE JACOBS

PENGUIN BOOKS

PENGUIN BOOKS
Published by the Penguin Group
Penguin Group (USA) LLC
375 Hudson Street
New York, New York 10014

USA · Canada · UK · Ireland · Australia
New · Zealand · India · South Africa · China
penguin.com
A Penguin Random House Company

First published in the United States of America by The Penguin Press,
a member of Penguin Group (USA) LLC, 2013
Published in Penguin Books 2014

Copyright © 2013 by StoryCorps, Inc.
Penguin supports copyright. Copyright fuels creativity, encourages diverse
voices, promotes free speech, and creates a vibrant culture. Thank you for
buying an authorized edition of this book and for complying with copyright
laws by not reproducing, scanning, or distributing any part of it in any form
without permission. You are supporting writers and allowing Penguin to
continue to publish books for every reader.

THE LIBRARY OF CONGRESS HAS CATALOGED THE HARDCOVER EDITION AS FOLLOWS:
Ties that bind : stories of love and gratitude from the first ten years of
StoryCorps / [edited by] Dave Isay with Lizzie Jacobs.
pages cm
ISBN 978-1-59420-517-0 (hc.)
ISBN 978-0-14-312596-9 (pbk.)
1. United States—Social life and customs—1971—Anecdotes.
2. United States—Biography—Anecdotes.   3. Interviews—United
States.   4. Oral history.   5. StoryCorps (Project)   I. Isay, David.
II. Jacobs, Lizzie.
E169.Z8T495 2013
973—dc23   2013017176

Printed in the United States of America
7   9   10   8   6

DESIGNED BY AMANDA DEWEY

Dedicated to the hundreds of staff who have given their time, talents, and heart to StoryCorps over the past decade. Mission-driven doesn't begin to cover it— you've proven yourselves mission-obsessed.

CONTENTS

TIES THAT BIND

INTRODUCTION

On October 23, 2003, the legendary oral historian Studs Terkel, ninety-one years old at the time, stood in front of a small sound studio aglow in the middle of Grand Central Terminal. "Today we shall begin celebrating the lives of the uncelebrated!" he said, pointing at our first recording booth. "We're in Grand Central Terminal. We know there was an architect, but who hung the iron? Who were the brick masons? Who swept the floors? These are the noncelebrated people of our country. In this kiosk, those anonymous people—the noncelebrated—will speak of their lives!"

Ten years and more than fifty thousand interviews later, StoryCorps stands as the largest collection of noncelebrated voices ever gathered in history—indeed, it stands as the largest collection of *any* voices ever gathered in history: almost one hundred thousand participants, recorded in more than a thousand locations and in all fifty states; eighteen terabytes of data, with hundreds of stories broadcast across the nation and around the world.

StoryCorps started out as a simple, if somewhat crazy, idea: build a soundproof booth where you can interview the most important person in your life with the help of a trained facilitator. The interview is structured to encourage people to dig deep—many think of it as "If I had forty minutes left to live what would I ask this person who means so much to me?" At the end of each session, the participants walk away with a CD copy of their interview, and StoryCorps sends another copy to the Library of Congress, where it becomes part of America's history. Someday, the great-great-great-grandchildren of StoryCorps participants will get the chance to meet their ancestors through this recording.

StoryCorps was built on a series of basic ideas I'd come to embrace in my twenties and thirties while working as a documentary radio producer: that a microphone gives people the license to ask questions of others that they wouldn't normally ask, and that being listened to reminds people how much their lives matter. StoryCorps is based on the belief that we can discover the most profound and exquisite poetry in the words and stories of the noncelebrated people around us, if we just have the courage to ask meaningful questions and the patience to listen closely to the answers.

Many of these ideas began taking shape for me twenty-five years ago, just after I'd graduated from college. In 1988, I was twenty-two years old and about to start medical school, when I was lucky enough to fall into public radio completely by accident. One afternoon I walked into a small shop on New York's Lower East Side owned by a married couple—both recovering heroin addicts with HIV—who told me about their dream of building a full-scale museum dedicated to stories of addiction before they died. While their task was clearly impossible, their spirits were remarkable. When I got home, I called every TV and radio station in the yellow pages to try to convince them to do a story about the pair. No one was the least bit interested—until I got to the news director of a local community radio station, a woman named Amy Goodman. She told me that it sounded like a good idea, but that she didn't have anyone available at the station to cover it. "Why don't you do it yourself?" she asked. So I took a recorder and interviewed the couple at their shop. When the story was aired on the station the next evening, a producer from NPR in Washington, DC, happened to be driving through town, heard the piece, and picked it up for national broadcast. I promptly withdrew from medical school to start down this new path. I had found my calling.

A few months before recording that story, I had also accidentally discovered that my father was gay. He and my mother had been married—extremely happily, I thought—for twenty-five years, and the revelation came as a shock. I was having a tough time dealing with the news—and with my dad. Once I started working in public radio, though, I thought I might be able to begin making sense of it all with a microphone and tape recorder. I wanted to understand more about my father and what his life had been like, but I wasn't ready to hear it from him.

One day my dad mentioned the Stonewall riots. I'd never heard of them, but I was intrigued and decided to learn more. I found out that on June 28, 1969, the police raided Stonewall Inn, a gay bar in Manhattan's Greenwich Village, and, with billy clubs drawn, they tried to shut it down. This was a common occurrence in gay bars all across New York City at that time—but on a series of nights that June, the patrons fought back. Nothing like it had ever happened before, and it sparked the modern gay rights movement in this country.

I decided to set off with a tape recorder to track down everyone I could find who might help me understand the riots, and what life was like for gay people in the years before. The microphone gave me the freedom to go places, meet people, and ask questions that otherwise would have felt completely out of bounds.

In New York's East Village, I found an elderly gay woman named Jheri living in senior housing just a few blocks from my apartment, who helped me understand the soul-numbing shame, fear, and abuse that ran rampant in the years before Stonewall. I met tough old Irish bartenders who exploded all of my preconceived notions of gay men. And I met Sylvia Rivera, who, as an eighteen-year-old drag queen and street kid, fought valiantly and viciously on the nights of the riots. No matter how many times she was clobbered with batons, she kept coming back for more. She was heroic and historic—today many consider her the Rosa Parks of the gay rights movement. Sylvia was the bravest and toughest person I had ever met.

These conversations turned my world upside down, and gave me a feeling of deep connection to a culture I'd known nothing about. By airing the program on public radio, I hoped the documentary might do the same for others. While there were some bumps along the way—I remember calling an arts editor of a New York tabloid and asking if she'd write a story about the documentary, since it was the first one ever made about the riots. "Sorry," she said. "We don't believe in homosexuality here"—the outpouring of response to the program was all I could have hoped for and more. I dedicated the documentary to my dad. We'd found common ground once again. It changed our relationship, and it changed my life.

I would go on to produce scores of radio documentaries about people living on the margins of society over the next fifteen years. I came to believe even more deeply in the lessons I learned from my Stonewall experience about the intimacy and immediacy of radio, the power of the human voice to transcend differences and divides, and the ability of a radio story to hit like an adrenalin shot to the heart when honestly and authentically told. I also saw, again and again, how affirming it was for people to be listened to, especially those who felt most silenced by the rest of society. Over the course of an interview I could see people's backs stretch and straighten—I would literally watch the experience make them stand taller.

The people I interviewed in those years—living in housing projects and forgotten small towns, working in hospitals and prisons, serving coffee at luncheonette counters, surviving in hospices and homeless shelters—inspired and moved me. They were some of the most powerful and important stories I could imagine—lives defined by courage, character, and conviction. People whose spirits could not be broken and whose sense of humor and hope never wavered. Time and again at the end of an interview, I'd have the same conversation:

"Have you ever told your story before?"

"No."

"Why not?

"No one ever asked."

Out of these and myriad other experiences and influences, I decided to undertake the fairly radical experiment of StoryCorps. Having seen the positive impact that participating in documentary work could have on people's lives, I wanted to open the experience to everyone. I hoped to create a project that was all about giving people the chance to interview one another, with only a secondary emphasis on editing stories for broadcast. In essence, StoryCorps flipped the purpose of traditional documentary work from an artistic or educational project created for the benefit of an audience into an experience principally focused on enhancing the lives of those recording the interviews.

Once StoryCorps opened, it quickly became clear that the idea was going to work. Participants told us that the forty minutes they spent in the booth were among the most important of their lives. People would sit down in front of the microphone and begin to weep even before the session began. In every interview, participants took the chance to talk about parts of their lives they had never discussed before. When participants passed away, we heard from family members that the CDs had become a cherished and singular record of their loved ones' voice, life, and spirit.

I wasn't sure when we launched StoryCorps whether we'd find any stories appropriate for radio broadcast coming out of these recording sessions—but I was wrong. We soon started editing brief audio segments from a handful of the interviews and airing them on public radio. We consider every interview session equally valuable and a potentially sacred moment in participants' lives, but we came to realize that some recordings had a universal quality that made them appropriate to share with a larger audience. We also realized that some of the interviews translated powerfully to the printed page— though not necessarily the same ones that worked on the radio—and started compiling our first StoryCorps book, *Listening Is an Act of Love*.

I think of StoryCorps as being in the wisdom collection business, and I have had the privilege over the past decade of immersing myself in the truths and life lessons that spring from the stories we record. Listening to the experiences of regular people living life to its fullest and exemplifying humanity at its finest has, time and again, stirred my soul and strengthened my faith in this nation and its people.

I think of Lynn Weaver, who recorded a StoryCorps interview about his father, Ted Weaver, in 2007 at the Martin Luther King, Jr., Center in Atlanta. Ted worked as a janitor in pre-civil-rights Knoxville, Tennessee. In Lynn's interview, which appears on page 172 of this book, he remembers a time he was struggling with high school algebra—and how one night his father stayed up until 4 a.m. teaching himself algebra from Lynn's textbook, so that he could in turn teach his son.

I was fortunate to be at a reception at the King Center where we listened to some of the stories recorded there, including Lynn Weaver's tribute to his dad. The next day, I received this e-mail:

> Mr. Isay,
>
> You will never know how honored and touched I was by the playing of the remembrance of my dad. After I got home, I realized that the evening of the StoryCorps reception was the anniversary of my father's death. Even in death, he continues to embrace me with his love. This project has touched me more than you will ever know.
>
> Lynn Weaver, chairman of surgery,
> Morehouse School of Medicine,
> Atlanta, GA

After you read Lynn's story, you'll understand why I think his father, Ted—a janitor from Knoxville, Tennessee—is the kind of man we should be building statues to and naming bridges after. He exemplifies America at its very best. The lessons we can all learn from a life like his are timeless and sacred.

This past decade's journey has been the most exhausting and exhilarating of my life. So much about StoryCorps goes against the grain of what can feel like a celebrity-choked culture. There were more than a few instances over the past ten years, especially when struggling to raise the money needed to keep StoryCorps afloat, that I'd think, *This isn't going to work, the whole idea is just nuts—maybe it's time to give it up!* But then I'd remember the small devoted army of facilitators fanned out across the country working tirelessly to lift up the voices of everyday people. Or our production team would walk into my office to play that week's NPR broadcast, and the truth and power of the story coming out of the speakers would jolt me back into reality.

Six months ago my seventy-eight-year-old dad, who seemed like the type to live to one hundred, was diagnosed with cancer. Nine days later, he died. It was June 28—the anniversary of the Stonewall riots. His doctor later described his illness as "a violent tornado that came out of nowhere and left total destruction in its wake." At 3:00 a.m. on the day after he passed, I listened for the first time to the StoryCorps interview we recorded together several years earlier. I had thought I couldn't believe in StoryCorps any more deeply than I already did, but hearing his voice speak to me from my computer twenty hours after his death, alone in my dark living room, knowing this was the way my two young children were going to get to know this man who meant so much to me—that was the moment the rubber hit the road, and I fully felt the significance of the work we've been doing.

The small team that launched StoryCorps in 2003 has now grown to become a staff of more than a hundred. We've recorded interviews in thousands of places—in cities, towns, and hamlets, and everywhere from a remote Alaskan fishing village to the White House. We've launched nine national initiatives, including StoryCorps Griot (a griot is a West African storyteller), which today stands as the largest collection of African American voices ever gathered. Our latest endeavor, StoryCorpsU, is a yearlong curriculum for high-needs schools that uses StoryCorps stories and teaches the StoryCorps interviewing method in order to help young people feel more connected to their teachers and each other, and help them recognize how much their lives matter. Early research shows the program's enormous potential for motivating, engaging, and inspiring kids at some of the toughest schools in the country.

But our work has really only just begun. It's our dream

that someday the StoryCorps interview method and the stories that we distill from these interviews will be woven into the fabric of American life and the lives of all Americans; that StoryCorps will grow into a sustaining national institution that reminds people that every life and every story matters equally. We hope, one day, to help foster an American culture that is a little more just and tolerant and that strives always to respect and nurture human dignity.

As I see it, one of the most important reasons to record a StoryCorps interview, and certainly the reason closest to my heart, is to honor the person or people to whom you feel most grateful. That person who stood by you during your darkest days, who recognized something special in you when no one else did; the person who rescued you or guided you or sustained you with their kindness, generosity, and strength of character. The family member, friend, teacher, neighbor, colleague—sometimes even stranger—with whom you feel a connection so powerful that the relationship can take on a sacred quality. These are the stories in *Ties That Bind*—a book of gratitude to mark the tenth anniversary of an undertaking built on human connection and kindness. Mother Teresa used to say, "We have forgotten that we belong to each other." This is a book that helps us to remember.

I hope that this collection—and every experience you've had or will have with StoryCorps—will do for you what it's done for me: that it will remind you it's never too early to say the important things to the people who matter to you most; that it will inspire you with all of the possibilities life presents when lived to its fullest; and that it will leave you feeling more connected, awake, and alive.

Dave Isay

AUTHOR'S NOTE

The following stories were edited from transcripts of StoryCorps interviews that typically run forty minutes. We aimed to distill these interviews without altering the tone or meaning of the original sessions. At times tense and usage were changed, and a word or two were added for clarity. We did not use ellipses to indicate omitted text; in the following pages ellipses indicate speech trailing off or a pause in conversation.

Words and phrases that read well are not always the strongest spoken moments, and the reverse is also the case. As a result, a story may vary from audio to print.

Participants gave permission for their stories to be published in this book, and each story was fact-checked.

"WE SAVED
EACH OTHER"

WIL SMITH, 43,

talks with his daughter,

OLIVIA SMITH, 16

Wil Smith: Four weeks after you were born, I was deployed. The hardest thing for me was leaving after spending just a few weeks with you. And I knew, had I stayed in the navy, I would always be leaving you. So I left the navy and applied to Bowdoin College and was accepted—though, at twenty-seven, I was considered a very nontraditional student.

Your mother had told me she was pregnant with you about a month after we stopped dating, and I had let her know that I would do whatever I had to do to care for you. And when you were ten, eleven months old, your mother was having a difficult time. She reached a breaking point, and it just became clear that being with me was the best thing for you at that time. So I took you to school with me.

It was very chaotic in the beginning. I actually thought that if Bowdoin knew I had you they wouldn't let me come to college, so I hadn't mentioned it to anyone. I was definitely the first single father raising a child on campus. I missed orientation because I was moving, so I showed up a day before classes and jumped right in the next day with no books and really didn't know how I was going to pay for them at the time.

I was able to get an apartment and a roommate and live off campus the first semester. I worked at Staples at night, cleaning, and I had to take you in with me to work sometimes and hide you in the closet. [*Laughs.*] Working, taking care of you, and playing basketball was wearing on me—I think I lost something like twenty-seven pounds in the first semester just from stress.

To be quite honest, I was not prepared for college. Had I not been able to kiss you good night every night before studying, I would not have had the strength to do it. There were times when the only way I could get through was to check in on you and see you sleeping, and then go back to my studies.

I thought that I could do it on my own, but it was getting very difficult. A woman who worked at Bowdoin reached out to me, and I told her all the things that were going on, and she helped me move to campus housing during the second semester. That was really the beginning of my college experience taking a turn for the better.

Olivia Smith: Were you ever embarrassed bringing me to class?

Wil: I don't think I was ever embarrassed—that's one of the few emotions that I didn't experience at that time. I was just glad that you were with me and that you were safe. I was very fortunate in that you were a relatively healthy child. You were quiet, didn't bother anyone—you were easy. And you adapted to school right away. I would take you to classes or give you crayons and things to do and you would just sit at a desk and do it.

My basketball teammates were my first babysitters. I remember coming from class and there were four giant guys over six feet and this eighteen-month-old who was tearing up the room. [*Laughter.*] That pretty much set the tone for how your experience was. I tell people all the time: Those guys on my team were the first people that I trusted with you.

My graduation day from Bowdoin is something I'll always remember. I carried you in my arms to get my diploma, and they called both of our names. All my classmates stood up and cheered—they gave me the only standing ovation of the day. It confirmed what I had endured for the past four years. It's no heroic thing that I did; I'm your father, and it was the right thing to do.

Olivia: So technically I already graduated from college . . .

Wil: Nice try. [*Laughs.*] The degree only has my name on it, so you've still got to go on your own.

Having you was a drastic change to my life, but it was the best thing that ever happened to me. I don't know if I ever told you this, but I felt like before you came along, my mother—my guardian angel, who passed away on my fifteenth birthday—was just looking down from heaven and got tired of me drifting through the universe and said, "God, please do something. Send that boy someone to take care of!"

I was so close to her, and I felt so empty when she passed away. And I've never really been able to explain this, but when I was in the delivery room when you were born, I physically felt something go into my heart. It was a feeling of completeness that I hadn't felt since my mother passed.

I was diagnosed with colon cancer two months ago, and now I'm watching you take care of me as if our roles were reversed. You've watched me at my weakest point—where no father wants to be—and you've been mature beyond your years. You're going to be fine. No matter what happens to me, I know you're going to be fine.

Olivia: It's hard for me, because I know you don't want me to be the one to take care of you, and you're probably scared about what's going to happen to me if I lose you. But that first week when I was home from school, I would cook you dinner and it made me happy being able to care for you, knowing that my whole life you were doing that for me. You're my rock.

Wil: I draw my strength from you. Being around you is what I've always lived for. And that's what's going to make me beat this. I've oftentimes referred to you as "my complex joy," and you've never stopped being that. I want you to know that you are the most important thing in my life, and you always will be as long as I'm on this earth. Everything else is a distant second. You were my mother's gift to me, and I believe that to this day.

RECORDED IN SHEFFIELD, MASSACHUSETTS, ON APRIL 24, 2012.

SUSAN MCCLINTON, 61,

talks with her husband,

PHILIP MCCLINTON, 63

Susan McClinton: When I was twenty-one, I came into the topless bar that you were bouncing. They were having amateur night, and I had decided to compete because I needed the prize money—I had two children to support.

Philip McClinton: When you came in, you immediately caught my attention. I just thought, *She doesn't belong in here.*

Susan: I remember at one point that night you said, "I'll keep an eye on you." And I think that was probably the beginning of our relationship. You always hear people talking about love at first sight. And for us, I think that really was the case. From the moment I saw you, I was just madly in love.

Philip: Well, you got me and all the baggage that came with me—I wasn't worth much at that point. I was into a number of things decent people just don't do.

Susan: You and I both had been on the wrong track. I was in an abusive marriage, and I was doing drugs and drinking a lot. If you hadn't come into my life at that particular moment, I think I would have ended up in a very bad place. But we knew if we wanted any kind of life together, we had to pull ourselves up and get out of those situations.

I remember at one point telling you that I had always enjoyed science. You said, "Well, why don't we just go back to school?" And I said, "You are out of your mind!" Because we didn't have any money to pay for tuition or anything like that. And I was just petrified to make that leap.

Philip: Neither one of us had anything but a ninth-grade education. I'd tried tenth grade three times and I couldn't cut it. Still, I said, "We should become biologists." We didn't think anyone would take us, but I said, "Call 'em and tell 'em we're grown and we need to do something." And Sul Ross State University accepted us on probation. I was thirty-nine, and you were thirty-seven. We were both working on biology degrees, and we took almost all of our courses together.

Susan: You didn't tell me until after we had been in school a while that you thought you wouldn't make it because you had never made good grades. But I told you, "Don't worry about it. I'll get you through it." And I tutored you in a lot of the harder subjects. We made little flash cards. In cell biology, we had to learn the Krebs cycle, and I drew a diagram and taped it up on the bathroom mirror so in the mornings you'd have to look at it and learn it from there.

We ended up with many more hours for our bachelor's degrees than most people do, because we just took every biology-related class there was. But then we decided that we needed to go farther and continue our research—

Philip: So we started our master's program. And, Susie, with your help I got through it all.

Susan: When we graduated, I don't think you could've wiped the smiles off our faces with a hand grenade. It was incredible. My life started out so bumpy, and after all the things we went through, I never thought we'd get college degrees.

You were always the one that said, "Why don't we try?" You know? You opened up such a world to me. I learned for the first time that I really was a person of worth—and I think you instilled that in me.

Philip: You figured out things on your own that you never dreamed you could do. And you did them so well. You turned into a very fine field biologist, and I'm proud of you.

Susan: You've always said we're not joined at the hip,

we're joined at the heart. We've called this a rescue romance, because we saved each other. We've been through rocky times, but the thing that we always fell back on was how much we loved each other.

RECORDED IN CODY, WYOMING, ON JULY 26, 2012.

RALPH CATANIA, 69,

talks with his "godson"
COLE WILLIAMS, 30

Ralph Catania: The first time I met you, Cole, you were one of my fifth grade students. And then I worked with you after school during seventh and eighth grade. It was during that time that I realized you were a pretty interesting and unique young man. You weren't a very outgoing child at that time—you were very conscious of what you had to say. But you were very caring.

So when your mom asked me if you could come stay with me, I didn't hesitate. How did you feel about coming to live with me?

Cole Williams: I guess I'd say I was scared. I'm a young black man. You're a white man. And I'm like, *I don't know anything about white people!* [*Laughs.*] I didn't know what kind of food you ate. I didn't know anything about your culture, your background. All I knew was that you were a nice teacher and you were going to take me in because my mother didn't have a place for me to stay. So I was very thankful for that.

When I came in, I didn't really have anything. And I wasn't quite sure how you transfer being a teacher and a student to developing something different, so it was nerve-racking for me.

And then, when I knew that I had a baby coming, I didn't quite know what you were going to say about that. I felt that you would probably put me out, because who's going to take in a teenager who's now having a child?

So I was really trying to keep it from you, honestly. And at the same time, I'm also trying to tell myself: *You're about to be a dad. Shouldn't you be preparing for this?* But how do you prepare for being a teenage father? There were no television shows about that, and there were no radio stations that talked about it.

Ralph: Well, when you did tell me you were going to be a father, I thought about it and just came to the conclusion that it was a no-brainer to say, *So you're going to be a father? We'll go from there.* And I think the thing that impressed me the most was your comment, "My son is going to know who his father is."

Cole: A lot of learning who I was had to do with becoming a father. And I think you played a huge role in that development, Ralph.

Nate's mom really believed that I was going to have a better life than she was, and eventually she decided I should take him. And it's funny how things pop into your mind, but I think the moment that I realized you were no longer my teacher was the very day that Nathan came home. You were no longer my math teacher, no longer my friend who would take me places or show me how to mow the lawn. You were going to help me learn how to raise my son. That's when it changed for me.

Ralph: Prior to having you and Nathan come into my life, I was working and taking care of myself. I had been married, but was single for a long period of time. I went from being a single person to having an instant family. I have a tremendous respect for parenthood now. It was a learning experience for both of us from the day Nathan was born.

Cole: I think the hardest part was just figuring out the day-to-day: waking up in the middle of the night, scrambling around trying to figure out the right temperature for milk. Who knew you had to find the right temperature for milk? I mean, I remember nights studying for an exam and he's sick and I'm trying to feed him at three o'clock in the morning. Or how to change a diaper—there was just a list of things that I didn't know . . .

Ralph: I think for both of us, Cole, for lack of a better term, it was like on-the-job training. [*Laughs.*] We had some rough moments, but there was always laughter.

It's truly been a blessing to watch this child grow up into the young man he is today. You've done a great job.

Cole: Well, I'll say to you this, Ralph: What you see in me is a reflection of what you put in me. One of the things that just lacked in my life was knowing that I could count on anyone to say and be where they're supposed to be. You provided that for me.

Ralph: You and Nathan changed my life. You made me realize that it's so much greater to love somebody, and that's something I will be forever grateful for.

Cole: And you've taught me that it's okay to be proud of who you are and it's okay to love. You've been able to provide

a sense of stability in my life where it's okay for me to be who I am, and it's okay to have a voice. And so today I say, "Thank you."

RECORDED IN ANN ARBOR, MICHIGAN, ON MARCH 2, 2010.

Cole Williams works in children's mental health and leads workshops on fatherhood.

KATE MUSICK, 43,

talks with her former student
HARLEÉ PATRICK, 15

Kate Musick: I remember the first time we met: You were coming in as a third grader, and you just looked so scared—this little girl with big, big eyes. You were behind, and it was my job to help improve your reading. You had such internal motivation to do well, but you had some difficulties maintaining focus. And when I stopped and sat down to talk to you, I thought to myself, *I'm going to have to keep an eye on her.*

Harleé Patrick: I didn't have the best home life. I always tossed between my grandma's house and my mom's house, and my mom wasn't really the mom you would want as a little girl—she was doing things that nobody was proud of, like drugs and things. She would want us sometimes, and then sometimes she wanted nothing to do with us. My dad wasn't really in the picture, and then when I was twelve, he passed away.

Kate: One of the things that I saw in you from the very beginning was a person that wanted to make her life better, even as an eight-year-old little kid. When people reached out to you, you chose to reach out and grab their hands, rather than push them away.

Harleé: I think one of the most difficult things for me and my brothers was when my mom would get locked up. She would get out and do something stupid and then go right back. Her not being there and then Dad not being there—it was like, *What do we do?*

Kate: There was one specific incident between your mom's stints in jail where you were very distraught. You and I sat down in the hallway, and you started talking about what you had witnessed the night before at your mom's trailer. And my heart was literally breaking.

Harleé: Honestly, all I really remember is going back and forth between Granny's house and Mom's house.

Kate: In a way, I'm glad you don't remember the specifics about that whole time period, because from what you described, they were some really horrific things for an eight-year-old child to be exposed to. I think there was some drug use and some very, very scary characters coming in and out of your life.

I wanted to do nothing more than to protect you. But I also knew that there were boundaries that teachers had to work within. And so I really tried to help you realize that what you were witnessing was not your fault and that we were there to help you always. We just tried to reassure you that you had a family outside of the house every day when you walked through the doors of T. C. Walker Elementary School. And I'm so glad that you got that message from us.

Harleé: To me, walking into T. C. Walker is like coming home again. Y'all thought of us students like family. And it's one of the best feelings you could ever have to feel like people care when you're going through rough times at home.

Kate: I think that what students don't realize is that, oftentimes, you guys help us teachers get through very difficult things as well. I was going through a divorce and had two small children, and I really don't think I would have been able to get through that without my students, because they lifted me up. My reason to get out of bed was to go to school, because I knew that you guys needed me.

One of the perks of my job is being able to maintain contact with you and to see where you're going. You're having success, and that's the best gratitude I could ever get as a teacher. Harleé, I want you to find happiness. And knowing you, I think happiness will be when you're able to help other people.

Harleé: I'm so thankful that you never gave up on me.

Kate: I never will give up on you. You're right here in my heart. That's where you're going to stay forever and always. Whenever you need me, I'm right here.

RECORDED IN HAMPTON, VIRGINIA, ON FEBRUARY 6, 2012.

Rami Aizic: Ever since I was ten or eleven years old, I knew that I needed and wanted to be a dad. I figured it would all just happen the way it happens to everybody else: I'd grow up, meet the girl of my dreams, get married, we'd have babies and live happily ever after. A little kink in that story was that when I was in my late twenties I realized I was gay. The whole format was drastically derailed. I really wanted a biological child, so I felt very much determined to figure out a way to have one.

I would be at parties, and I would just say, "Oh, by the way, if you know of any women, gay or straight, who would be interested in having a child with me in some capacity, give them my number"—which would shock my friends. And after about three years, I got one of the strangest phone calls of my life.

My dear friend Scottie said, "This is going to sound a little bit strange, but I met this woman. Her name is Robin— she's really nice and funny and bright, and she is interested in having a child. I told her about you, and I want you to give her a call." So, after lifting my jaw off the floor, I said, "Okay, I will."

I called you and left a message, saying something along the lines of, "Hi, Robin. I'm a friend of Scott Schwimer, and he told me you might be interested in having a baby with me. So give me a call back." And that was the beginning.

Robin Share: I'd always imagined that I would have kids, too. But I didn't even entertain ideas of motherhood—or even marriage, really—until I was probably thirty-seven or thirty-eight, and it hit me: *I don't have a boyfriend or a husband, and I really want to have kids!* I did look into adoption, but I think I was still holding out for Mr. Right. I wasn't really looking for a love match; I was looking for someone to have a family with. An anonymous sperm donor was an option, but I had this idea in my head that I wanted my child to have a father. That was paramount for me.

Rami: So you came over, and it was a strange, yet surprisingly pleasant visit. I remember us talking pretty bluntly about what we were looking for and whether or not to go forward with this.

Robin: It didn't take long. By the third or fourth time meeting, we were pretty sure.

Rami: We'd put together this informal family pact as to what would happen to the child if one or the other of us would die, what would happen if we both died, who would get custody, and financial obligations.

I thought we should see a family therapist, to see if we were missing any big issues in this idea of having a family. I remember meeting you in the waiting room for our final visit, and you seemed kind of fidgety and tense. We got into the therapist's office and you blurted out, "I've met someone, and I think I need to stop this whole process."

I was devastated. But you were still hoping for Mr. Right to do this the traditional way. I remember wanting to be so angry with you and yet completely understanding what you were saying. I wanted to be happy for you. But initially I was in shock, and I just wanted to run away from the world.

A few weeks went by, and there was a message from you on the machine. I remember calling you back and you said something along the lines of, "This guy is a very nice guy, but he's not for me."

Robin: He wasn't Mr. Right. *You* were Mr. Right.

Rami: At that point, I knew: You wanted the best for this child above and beyond anything else. So we went straight ahead, because a) I didn't want to lose you again for some other guy that might come along, and b) I just knew you had to be the right person.

Robin: And then on November 9, 1998—*boom.* I got pregnant.

Rami: I remember coming home and on the porch was a little bag with a rubber ducky, two cigars, and a little note from you. That's how you let me know.

Robin: After Bailey was born, I was thinking, *This man is going to be in my life for the rest of my life.* The implications were huge, and it was scary.

I think for the first year or two I was waiting for the other shoe to drop, but by now I've stopped waiting, because I know it's not going to.

Rami: For that first year, we decided that you would stay home from work, but my concern was *Would I ever bond with this child anywhere near as much as you have?* And then, when I would get her, your mother would always step in and say, "When are you going to bring her back to us, Rami?"

Robin: It was always a challenge with my mother—I had to keep repeating to her, "He's not stealing her! I want them to bond." And I remember writing you a Father's Day card or a birthday card early on that said, "One day, she will see you across the room and come running to you with her arms out, saying, 'Daddy!'" And she does that all the time now.

I envy her, because I didn't have that kind of relationship with my father. My parents divorced when I was four and a half, and I had almost no relationship with my biological father. So when you throw Bailey up in the air and catch her, and when you taught her how to ride a bike . . . I'm just so happy. And Bailey knows there's so much love between us— she knows she has loving parents who love each other, too.

Rami: I look at you pretty much every day, thinking, *How did I get so lucky?* Because there really isn't a better mother that I know. In every way. And the fact that we've worked as hard as we've worked, and yet it doesn't seem like work. What we do for each other is such a great complement. We have given our child a legacy that I'm sure she'll be very proud of one day.

RECORDED IN SANTA MONICA, CALIFORNIA, ON NOVEMBER 12, 2007.

ROBERT SANCHEZ, 41,

talks with his friend
FELIX APONTE, 28

*Robert served fifteen years in prison for a
nonviolent first-time drug offense.*

Robert Sanchez: You were coming to a job placement center
where I worked as a case manager. I was thirty-five years
old, and was home from prison maybe two or three years at
that time. You were about twenty years old, and immediately
I saw that you were a pain in the ass. But you were a pain in
the ass who wanted something more—you just didn't know
how to get it. So you took a liking to me and I took a liking
to you.

Felix Aponte: Well, I could tell off the bat that you were like me. We haven't lived the same life, but once you do time it's like—

Robert: —there's a bond.

Felix: Yeah. And we clicked because I could see you were going to tell me the truth. You're one of those people that if I call, you always come to help.

Robert: Four years after I came home, in 2005, I got hit with kidney disease. I noticed it when I started to get these huge headaches. I've never been drunk in my life, I don't get high, and I don't use any type of drugs. So when I got these headaches, I said, *Well, it has to be just that I'm stressed out.* My mom was an alcoholic, and I was concerned about her drinking problem, so I felt like maybe that was what was going on. And I kept ignoring it.

Eventually the doctor told me that I had an aggressive form of kidney disease, and what usually takes people five to ten years to go from a healthy kidney function to no kidney function took just a year for me. And when I finally realized that I had this terminal illness, everything crashed.

I couldn't do my job correctly and so I just quit out of the blue. I lost my apartment. I was lonely. I was sick. I had nowhere to go. I went through this whole emotional roller coaster.

And then one day you called me. You said, "Yo, what's

up?" And I'm like, "Who's this?" You said, "Me. You forgot me?"

Felix: You told me that you had kidney disease. And I was like, "You don't got nobody that'll donate?" Nobody in your family stepped up. So I was like, "So what about me?" And you were like, "Yeah, whatever, Felix." You just kept on brushing it off.

Robert: Part of why I kept brushing you off was because I felt like you had so much shit going on. How were you going to fit that into getting back on your own two feet? And how do you ask somebody for a kidney?

Felix: You always looked out for my best interests. So I said, *He needs help. I'm going to help him.* I'm in good health. Plus, I wanted to do something good in my life for the first time, you know? All I've done is mischief.

Robert: I kept saying, "Felix, come on, I don't want to talk about that." But you just never wavered.

At our last checkup, we're sitting down and they're checking me and they're checking you. And you said, "Look—I want to do this." And that's when I knew it was real.

Now, for the first time in my forty-one years, I feel that my life finally belongs to me. It doesn't belong to the prison system anymore. It doesn't belong to my illness. I feel like I won the lotto because you saved my life—that was my million dollars. I'm a very lucky man.

Our relationship has been more than just two friends—I hope you know that. You gave me my life back.

RECORDED IN NEW YORK, NEW YORK, ON FEBRUARY 1, 2010.

FELIZ APONTE *(left)*
AND ROBERT SANCHEZ.

GUS HERNANDEZ, 41,

talks with his employer and friend,

SIDDIQI HANSOTI, 52

Gus Hernandez: I grew up here in Salinas—been here for most of my life. Much of the county was small towns, but in 1991 or 1992 we had a boom in the real estate business, and I saw that as a big opportunity. So I jumped on the wagon and sold real estate and home loans.

But then real estate crashed. I lost work, the loan agency foreclosed on my house, and I got an eviction notice. I said, *What's going to happen now?* For the first time in my life I didn't have any answers. We stayed at the house a few more days but every knock on the door felt like they were coming to take us out. So one day I told my wife, "Let's just go. I can't live like this for another day."

We spent a couple of nights at local motels and ran out of

money. Then we spent a couple of nights in the car. I called everywhere I could possibly think of and asked for help or shelter for my family—and, to my amazement, there were no shelters that would take a family in Monterey County. I was in shock. I told my wife, "Look, we can't stay in the car anymore. We have the kids. Let's call around and see what we can find." And I started looking through the yellow pages.

I found the El Dorado Motel, and you answered the phone. When I came in I said, "Look, I've got fifty dollars in my pocket and I'm looking for a room." You gave me the key and said, "You can pay me on Friday. I trust you."

Siddiqi Hansoti: I observe your family, and I think you are a nice man. You're a soft-speaking guy. And sometimes I come to your room and we talk about what you are doing, how you're doing, how you became in trouble and lost everything. We talked about business and about our kids. How many days you stay in motel?

Gus: Three weeks. And then I said, "I don't have any more money, and I don't want to owe you any money, so I'm going to leave."

Sid: But I think, *I need a handyman. He's not a professional, but he can learn very fast.* So I give you the job, and you work with me and you stay in my motel also.

Gus: I'd never done it in my life! [*Laughs.*] But I just

needed a little bit of help, and you lent me a hand at a time that nobody did.

Sid: Well, America is the land of opportunity. I came here from Bombay in 1990. I moved all over; then I bought this motel in 2007. I *own* this business—that's why I love America. My family survived with this business, so I'm happy to help.

Gus: We get exposure to different walks of life in this motel. We sort of watch for each other: If we know that somebody doesn't have any food, everybody will pitch in. And if somebody needs a ride, they actually come to the office and we'll find them a ride. If they're falling behind, we hand out a package with all the numbers to call to get some help so they can stay and have a roof for the time being.

Sid: We all live like a family, actually.

Gus: When I had money, I had a lot of friends. But when I didn't, you were there. I once told you, "You don't mix business with friends." So when I'm working for you, I'm your employee. But after work, I'm your friend.

SIDDIQI HANSOTI *(left)*
AND
GUS HERNANDEZ.

RECORDED IN SALINAS, CALIFORNIA,
ON MARCH 13, 2009.

PAUL CROWLEY, 60,

talks with his friend

DREAMER, 69

*Dreamer runs a barbershop in a trailer outside of a VA hospital,
where he gives free haircuts to veterans.*

Paul Crowley: When I first showed up at your shop, I was
totally out of hope—my life had fallen apart completely. I
had lost my family, and I had totally alienated my friends. All
my property, all my money—everything was gone.

I hadn't shaved in a couple weeks, my hair was filthy, my
clothes were filthy—*I* was filthy. But getting a haircut from
you made me feel, for lack of a better word, normal—which
I hadn't felt in a long, long time.

Dreamer: When I first saw you, I saw a guy that could at
some point rise above it. And I just felt that I could help you.

I had started cutting hair in Arizona, where I grew up, and
I got really good at it. And so after serving in the National

Guard during Vietnam, I wound up here in Los Angeles and made my career as a barber in West LA. You try to do the best you can with whatever you got, and I wanted to figure out a way to treat vets with the courtesy and respect that every human being deserves. That's when I got the trailer and started giving them free haircuts.

Paul: I remember when I first looked in your eyes. I had a feeling: *Okay, this gentleman is for real.* The shop became a safe haven.

I'm still here, and I feel honored to be able to help you out. Somebody comes up, the first thing is we make them feel comfortable: "Hey, how you doing? Need a haircut? C'mon in! What branch of service were you in?"

Dreamer: The first thing is treat them with respect. Just make guys feel that they're appreciated. It's not really about a haircut. And whatever you got, we'll make a deal for it. Rubber-band balls, pebbles, rocks, washers . . .

Paul: I've never seen you turn anybody away. These veterans walk in feeling down and defeated, and with some kind words, a few jokes, and a haircut, they walk out feeling like better men. They come in dragging and they leave with their head high.

It's amazing to me to see the guys that come in, and then after they've been in a few times they're going out to look for work. And then they come in with a suit and the haircut you had given them and you can't even recognize them compared to the day they walked in there.

You impressed me from the very start, and I respect what you have imparted to me. It's what has made me into a better person.

Dreamer: Thank you, buddy.

RECORDED IN LOS ANGELES, CALIFORNIA, ON FEBRUARY 1, 2012.

PAUL CROWLEY *(left)*
AND DREAMER.

ZACHARIAH FIKE, 31,

talks with his "second mom,"
ADELINE ROCKKO, 84

Zachariah Fike: For Christmas 2009, my mom bought me a Purple Heart she found in a local antique shop in Watertown, New York. I remember unwrapping it on Christmas Day, and it was in a beautiful, pristine case. I could tell it was well cared for. I looked on the back and there was a name engraved on it: Corrado A. G. Piccoli. As soon as I saw it, I knew I had to find who this guy was and why this medal was in an antique shop.

I invested three days into the project, and everything was coming together for me—I found his high school yearbook, his enlistment records, and some family information—but I had to leave for deployment to Afghanistan. So I put the search on hold for a year.

On September 11, 2010, I was wounded. I was hit by a

rocket while sleeping and received some shrapnel through the back of my leg. I was very fortunate to walk out of that room and I'm lucky to be here today.

When I got home around Christmas of 2010, I saw the medal, and I knew I had to pick up the search again. Corrado's funeral service had been at St. Anthony's Church in Watertown, so I stopped by and met with a nun, and she knew Mary Piccoli, one of Corrado's sisters. Within ten minutes I was sitting down with Mary at her kitchen table. I told her the story, and she didn't say much. But on the way home, I received a phone call from you.

Adeline Rockko: The very first thing I said to you was, "Who are you, and what are you doing with my brother's medal?" I flooded you with questions—*bam, bam, bam*, one right after the other. But you were stalwart.

Zachariah: I tried to be as professional as I could. I represented myself as Captain Zack Fike of the United States Army, and I said that my mom had found this medal in an antique shop. But you immediately started blasting me with, "What antique shop? What do you mean? Who are you? Where do you live?" And I answered your questions to the best of my ability.

Adeline: After the conversation ended, I walked away from the phone and I said, *Oh my God—he's such a nice young* man. *He's returning our medal, and I treated him this way!* So I called you right back again, apologized, and thanked you.

This medal was very precious to my parents. On special occasions my mother would take it out and reminisce. Every once in a while she would let us hold it in our hands, and then she would put it back in the trunk in her bedroom. It was just a little gold heart with Washington's picture on it, and a purple ribbon. For a while I thought, *What's the significance of this medal?* But as I grew older and missed my brother more and more, I realized that this is the only tangible thing that we had left, and that's why my mother held it so dearly to her heart.

You called me on a Wednesday, and that Friday night was our first meeting. I drove for seven hours up to Watertown in the middle of winter and met with you at your mother's home. I knew it was in good hands when you brought the medal down from your bedroom and I saw that it was in the very same box that I had last seen it in—in just absolute perfect condition.

My brother was my mentor. He taught me how to speak English—he was two and a half years old when we came across the North Atlantic from Italy. He was the translator, the interpreter, the leader—he just forged ahead, and we all followed him. He was the oldest in the family, the firstborn son. I was the firstborn daughter. And there are four other daughters and another son behind us.

When he went into the service in 1942, I took the role that he had: I became the translator and leader in the family. I was the one who wrote the family letters to him while he was in the service.

October 7, 1944, was the day that he died. And October 29 was the day that we got the telegram that Corrado had been killed. It was my sister Elma's birthday. We didn't want to have a celebration, but my mother said, "Go ahead. Life goes on." So that's what we did—we had the cake. I was only seventeen when he died.

We were very fortunate that you were the one who ended up with the Purple Heart, and we thank you very much for returning it to us. It represents a lot of memories, and a lot of what used to be and never would be again.

I often wonder how long the medal had been in that antique shop, and how many people passed by it. To think that it was for sale . . . We still have no idea how it got there, but we're very thankful that it got into your hands.

Zachariah: I think the most significant thing for me is transitioning from honoring Corrado to having you bring me into your family.

Adeline: Well, that was only normal. That's what Italian families do, and you went through an awful lot finding us.

Zachariah: Corrado has taught me a lot about history and what it means to be a good man and serve your country. And he's ultimately brought me another mom and another family. I think we all owe that to him.

RECORDED IN NEW YORK, NEW YORK, ON APRIL 10, 2012.

JOSE "PEPE" NORIEGA, 67,

talks to

LYNN GUARCH-PARDO, 55,

about her father, Jorge "George" Guarch

*Pepe came to the United States as part of Operation Pedro Pan,
a clandestine program that brought more than fourteen thousand
children from Cuba to Miami in the early 1960s.*

Jose "Pepe" Noriega: After Fidel Castro took over Cuba, my
father said that he wanted my brother and me to come to the
United States. My father saw no future for us in Cuba—
people started to lose their businesses, and a lot of people went
to jail. So we had to move.

Three or four days after my father started procuring nec-
essary documentation for our passports, we had a seat on Pan
American Airways to leave. My brother was sixteen years old
at the time, and I was seventeen. He left on the tenth and I on
the eleventh of October 1961. Maybe four or five other kids
in the Pedro Pan operation came with me.

It was like one life ended and another one began. We were to be away from our family for a long time—or maybe never see them again—so it was very, very tough.

In Cuba, my dad had said to me, "When you go there, you're going to ask for George." So I came out of the walkway from the plane in Miami, and there was a policeman standing at the end of it. I asked for George, and he said, "You cannot miss him. He's over there waiting for you guys to get out." He was leaning against a column, waiting for all the kids who came with me on the plane.

From the airport, George took us to your house, and your mom prepared for us peanut butter and jelly sandwiches. And after that night, I saw George almost every day.

George was unique. He had curly hair and a gravelly voice, and I thought he was the Second Coming of Jesus Christ, because he knew everything! [*Laughter.*] He was a heart walking on two legs. He cared about the well-being of every kid. He said we were his family—his words: *family*.

Later on in life, we would have lunch once a week. So Wednesdays at twelve o'clock either he would go to my office or I would go to his place of work. We'd go to one of the restaurants close by and for an hour we'd talk about everything—from baseball to politics, your family, my family, to whatever topic that would come up. And we did that for years.

I enjoyed George's friendship for many, many years. But

then one day when I went to pick him up for lunch, they said he had died the day before, just crossing the street. It was heartbreaking.

I think about George a lot. When I tell stories to my wife and my kids about him, I can be talking for a week, you know? He would make any kind of sacrifices for the people he knew needed something . . .

He was one of my best friends. I've got five fingers, and I only can count my good friends with one hand. And George was number one. I still miss him.

RECORDED IN CORAL GABLES, FLORIDA, ON DECEMBER 7, 2010.

Jose "Pepe" Noriega passed away on January 12, 2014.

SCOTT MACAULAY, 49

Scott Macaulay: In September of 1985, when I was twenty-six, my folks decided to get divorced. I was taught that to be a good son, I needed to be supportive and loving to each parent and to my siblings. But nobody was talking to anybody. If you were nice to one parent, the other one would get mad with you. So when October came, I thought, *What's going to happen at Thanksgiving?* And the thought of being home alone—or anywhere alone—on Thanksgiving, I just did not like that.

Thanksgiving is not gifts or fireworks or hoopla. It's a meal around a table to give thanks for the blessings you have, and you really can't do that by yourself and have much fun at it. So I decided I was going to do my own thing and provide Thanksgiving dinner for other people stuck home in the same boat.

I put an ad in the local paper: If people thought that they would find themselves alone on Thanksgiving and they didn't want to be, give me a call and I would make a Thanksgiving dinner. So that's what I did—twenty-five years ago this year.

It went well; a few people came, and they had a good time. I was nervous about making a mess out of the food and disappointing people. But the food was okay, and I didn't burn anything.

Last year, eighty-four people showed up. Sometimes they're new to town, sometimes they're recently divorced or recently lost a spouse. I've had people that were new to the country, and they didn't speak any English but they enjoyed my Thanksgiving dinner. I have poor people, people that come from AA, old people. Also, not counted within that number: I always feed the police. The fire department and the ambulance people are in buildings that have kitchens and can have their own Thanksgiving dinner amongst themselves, but the police officers are in their cars, driving around town on call.

Two years ago a woman with Parkinson's disease came who was not good on her feet. She had been in the nursing home for seven years and had never been out, and I think she was sick of it. Somebody had told her about the dinner, and she decided that she was coming. So she hired an ambulance company to come and get her, at two hundred dollars plus mileage. She had a great time, and she cried when the ambulance guys came to get her. She didn't want to go home.

Most of the people that come don't know who I am. They know there's some skinny guy in the kitchen, but they don't know my name. I think the theme of my life, and everything I do, could be quoted after an old hymn called "Brighten the Corner Where You Are." I hope my legacy would be that I came into the world, I brightened the corner, and then I quietly left the world unnoticed.

RECORDED IN MELROSE, MASSACHUSETTS, ON OCTOBER 21, 2010.

MARVIN GOLDSTEIN, 66,

talks to his son,

ERIC GOLDSTEIN, 40

Marvin Goldstein: My earliest memory was when I was about three. It was 1944 or 1945, and we had an apartment in Williamsburg, Brooklyn, on the fifth floor. My parents at that point in time slept in the living room on a pullout sofa, and I slept in the bedroom. And the windows did not have window guards. I was sleeping, and sometime in the late afternoon, I woke up from a dream. I had a friend across the way in another apartment building, and for some reason I thought that he was calling me. So I went to the window, opened it, and started calling him.

I leaned out, but my center of gravity was no longer in the apartment and I fell five stories. But I was caught by a barber—Sal Mauriello. He was coming home early that day when he heard a woman scream. She pointed up to the window and he saw me dangling by one hand. So he took off his coat and I fell into his arms.

Eric Goldstein: He used his jacket as a net to catch you? Amazing!

Marvin: Yes. And good thing he was a good catch! He took me around the corner into an obstetrician's office, and there were many women in there. He had me in his arms and he said, "This boy just fell out of a fifth-story window!" And all the women were yelling and screaming.

The doctor called for an ambulance. Everyone in the building and across the street knew each other, and so one woman ran and got my mother. They took me to Greenpoint Hospital, which is no longer in existence, and they found that there was no trauma beyond I might have fractured my nose.

I became very popular in the neighborhood. My mother's name was Blanche, and I was known as Blanche's Son Who Fell Out of the Window. I would walk down the street and people would stop me and say, "Are you Blanche's Son Who Fell Out of the Window?" And it became routine. That stayed with me for a very, very long time.

Eric: What ever happened to Sal?

Marvin: He closed his shop and moved to California. For

years my mother communicated with Sal—she would wish him a happy holiday and so on—but then she lost touch with him. Many, many years later, in 1988, we were coming home from visiting your grandparents in Florida. And while we were taking the suitcases out of the car, your brother went into the house. Then he came running out and said, "Dad, you're not going to believe this—there's an article about you in the *Daily News*!" So we got the *Daily News*, and there was a headline that said, "Desperately Seeking Marvin."

Well, it turned out that every Passover holiday Sal would say, "I wonder what happened to Marvin Goldstein." So finally his daughter said, "Dad, let's see if we can find out." So she called the *New York Daily News,* and they wrote this article. They then arranged for Sal and his wife to come for a meeting. It was a glorious reunion. It was absolutely thrilling to see Sal, the man who saved my life. We hugged, we kissed, and we went to the building and the *Daily News* took photographs.

His wife said that this was one of the most important days in his life. And I said, "Well, his being there for me, of course, was one of the most important days in my life!" And when I looked up at the height from where I lived, I said, "Oh my God—what a courageous man to put his own life at risk!" 'Cause God only knows, I could have fallen on him and killed him.

He told Mom and me that he actually kept the jacket with the blood from my nose, and he never cleaned it. For many years he wanted to know if I was okay, and he was just so, so happy that we were together again.

RECORDED IN NEW YORK, NEW YORK, ON APRIL 1, 2009.

MARVIN GOLDSTEIN *(left)*
AND ERIC GOLDSTEIN.

"BEEN THROUGH BATTLES"

STEFAN LYNCH, 40,

remembers his family to his friend

BETH TEPER, 43

Stefan Lynch: My mom and dad both came out when I was pretty young. They stayed friends but separated, and I lived mostly with my dad when I was younger.

Because we'd essentially been disowned by our biological family, my family were these mostly gay guys, whom I called my aunties. For a lot of these men, I was the one kid that they could feel comfortable being around—they could be themselves. And I was the one kid they got to have in their lives, because many of them were alienated from or rejected by their families, too. They were wonderful—they were my babysitters and the guys who took the pictures at my birthday parties. It was a really amazing world, but it came crashing down starting in '82.

I remember when I was about ten, we were on Fire Island and one of my aunties, Steve, was lying on the beach listening to his Walkman, and he was covered in these purple spots. I remember asking my dad, "What's wrong with Steve?" And my dad said, "Oh, he has this skin cancer called Kaposi's sarcoma." I said, "What is that?" And my dad said, "Well, nobody really knows, but there are some gay men that are getting it." Within two months, Steve was dead. He was probably twenty-two or twenty-three. And then it was pretty much a succession of deaths in my family throughout the next decade.

My stepdad, Bill, was there for ten of my first fifteen years, and he was the only other person I consider a parent. He was a microbiologist, and I was really into science, so I'd go over to his lab and he'd show me his weird lab equipment. One spring, I remember he got an old terrarium and we threw a bunch of food into it and let it mold for three months. He told me about how mold works, and then we took it into his lab and looked at it under the microscopes.

Bill was very healthy, and then one day he wasn't. I remember he was coughing for two weeks and just getting scareder and scareder—he so wanted to believe that it was just a bad cold. Bill had actually just gotten a grant to do research on retroviruses, and he was studying HIV in his lab. So he knew that this could be the end, but he didn't want it to be. Within three weeks, he died, too. That was 1987.

In '91, I took a break from college to take care of my dad full-time while he was dying. It was really grueling. I remember I called my auntie Eddie when I was exhausted and just needed a break. I said, "Can you help?" And within a week he'd organized forty people to do round-the-clock shifts to take care of my dad up until he died. I was nineteen. At that point everyone had died except for a handful of stragglers, who I now hold near and dear to my heart.

AIDS was horrific, but one of the things that gay men did very well, and still do very well, was to resist through joy. I had this amazing family—even though nobody outside my community could see it—and there was a lot of love. They modeled for me how to survive an epidemic, even if you were dying while doing it.

A couple months ago, I took my twenty-month-old son, Micah, to meet my auntie Eddie. It was really special to have this little person meet Ed, who had known me since I was just a couple years old, and who was the only other person in the room with me and my mom when my dad died.

To get to introduce Micah to Auntie Eddie—one of my only aunties who survived—was more than special. It felt like a miracle.

RECORDED IN SAN FRANCISCO, CALIFORNIA, ON NOVEMBER 25, 2012.

JOSH KLIPP, 39,

talks with his brother

LUKE KLIPP, 34

Josh is a transgender male.

Josh Klipp: There are four of us. We have an older sister and a younger brother, and you and I are in the middle. We had a very tense relationship growing up—I didn't get what it was about at the time, but I was just insanely jealous of you. I was really jealous of the opportunities that presented themselves to you that I didn't get, like playing football. God, what I would've given to play football! [*Laughs.*]

When we lived just outside of Detroit, in the blue house on Allen Street, there was a giant playground across the street with a baseball diamond. There was this pickup game happening, and I wanted you to play. And I was so mad at you because here you were, strong, broad shouldered—the *boy*—

and you just weren't interested! I just felt like you had every-thing I'd wished I had, and you weren't using it the way I would have if I were you.

I remember once when I was home for the weekend from college, there was a dance at the high school. I was giving you all kinds of crap about asking Katie to go, because I wished that *I* could have asked a girl to a dance when I was in high school—and here you had a girl who liked you! But finally, you just told me to shut up. Then you said, "I think I'm gay . . ." And I felt like such an a-hole, because I was doing to you what I didn't want done to me—pressuring you to be a way that you're not.

From that point on, I was like, *Okay, how can I support you? How can I be the best sibling to you that I can be now that I know?* It just flipped the whole script.

Luke Klipp: You became my ally and my closest support—especially as I came out to Mom and Dad. And then, later, you told me, "Luke, I think I want to be a boy." And I re-member thinking, *That sounds right.*

Josh: A friend of mine was getting married down in Big Sur, and you had come with me. I decided that this would be the weekend to try out my new name. But it was miserable. I was stumbling over my name all day. I felt scared and trapped, like people were looking at me. I remember just wanting one moment of something familiar. And so I said to you, "Can you say my old name just once?"

Luke: I wanted to be able to keep you safe. And I wanted people to accept you just as you were.

You know, for almost my entire life I've perceived that you've got things figured out and that you've got a clear direction that you're driving toward. That's something I've always envied.

Josh: You think that I have things all figured out, but it's not even close. I feel at ease with you. I feel like I can make a mistake and you're still going to forgive me. And you make me think about things in ways I haven't before.

You're engaged now, and I'm engaged now. But you and I are a team. I remember when I was maybe sixteen, Mom said to me, "You should be nicer to your brother because someday you might need him to fix your car." And I thought, *I don't think Luke is ever going to be able to fix my car!* [*Laughs.*] But Mom meant it's important to have each other around, and she's right.

Luke: I've always respected and admired you—your tenacity, your ferocity, and your willingness to put everything on the line for your vision, whatever that is.

Do you still envy that I was born a boy and you weren't?

Josh: No. What really changed that for me was what you

said to me when I was transitioning—"and no offense to Dad," which is how you prefaced it—that I taught you everything you know about being a man. I couldn't have a better brother, and I couldn't be more proud of you and what a great man you are.

RECORDED IN SAN FRANCISCO, CALIFORNIA, ON DECEMBER 2, 2012.

JOSH KLIPP *(left)*
AND LUKE KLIPP.

GEOFF DENNIE, 29,

talks with his brother
GREG DENNIE, 28

Geoff Dennie: Remember when we had a paper route? We had to wake up early, and there'd be those days when we'd both walk out of our rooms and see each other in the hallway, and you could tell—*this guy's looking for a fight!* [*Laughter.*] We'd go out and get the papers and start bumping each other and knocking each other's rubber bands off. And then on the route there would just be an outright fight. Later, we'd be like, "Hey, I'm sorry about that." I think that was one of the things that's made us close over time. We used to fight all the time and then—

Greg Dennie: —immediately make up. No matter what happened. And even as much friction as there was on the paper routes, in the wintertime I always remember walking down the street and seeing your pigeon-toed steps in the snow, and in my head, I was like, *I want to be just like him. I'm going to follow—literally—in his footsteps.* But my feet go outward and I looked like an idiot following these awkward footsteps.

Geoff: Someone should have explained to you that it was a metaphor. [*Laughter.*]

Greg: I know! And I didn't learn to stop following you until high school, really. There's something very comforting about being with an older brother who just leads the way constantly. I always was very much like a loyal German shepherd, and I never really had to think for myself until you went to college.

Geoff: I got bad news about my heart when I was twenty-one. The odds were not in my favor—even with a transplant. It was a coin toss whether I'd make it ten years . . . and I was scared.

Greg: I was in the marines training in North Carolina when I got a message about your heart failure, and I almost broke down and cried on the spot in front of all the other marines. After that, I tried not to think about it much.

I never asked what was going on—I just preferred to be in the dark. Mom would call me on the phone and say, "You know, things are getting worse." I'd kind of be like, "Why did you tell me that? Why couldn't you just let me be the little brother?" I constantly hid behind ignorance to cope.

Geoff: And I was trying to prove myself. My mentality was, *if I quit doing the things I loved doing, then the disease won.*

Greg: You ran the Marine Corps Marathon with the pacemaker in your chest, and that, for me, was proof that there was nothing wrong. I bragged so much to my friends about your accomplishments—which were considerable even for a healthy person.

But there were times when I'd say to myself, *What if you died? Who do I have that I can talk to the way I talk to you?* I've never had the in-depth conversations I have with you with anybody else. I'd lose my filter for the world if you were gone.

So I'd pray for death to just stay away one more day. Like, *Well, if he could just make it to be the best man at my wedding . . . if he could just be there to hold my firstborn child . . .*

Geoff: Then, last spring, my defibrillator started to run out of batteries, and they had to do a procedure to take it out and put a new one in. And when they saw my heart, they told me it didn't really look like it should if I had the disease they thought I had. The last time I was at the hospital, the doctors said they wouldn't have known I had had the disease if they hadn't read it on my sheet.

Greg: I remember talking on the phone to our little brother, Robin, and he was jubilant—I've never heard him that happy before. He was just kind of like, "Geoff's cured! He's not going to die!" But then, when I talked to you, you were like, "We'll just play it by ear—things seem good now but we can't get carried away."

Geoff: Not that long ago, I wanted to do things at extremes and thought of life as a heroic mythic journey, but now it's nice to be able to think of it as just one more day and be okay with it. Every day is like a bonus day.

Greg: Life is in no way what I thought it was supposed to be. When I was younger and more willing to believe things absolutely, I thought that I was invincible and that my family was invincible—that *you* were invincible. Robin and I would refer to you as Superman.

Now we don't fight with each other anymore, we don't run with each other anymore, but we talk more, and I feel

more. Just your presence is reaffirming, and I admire the way you're able to work through things. To me, that's as close as you get to Superman.

RECORDED IN NEW YORK, NEW YORK, ON OCTOBER 27, 2012.

GEOFF DENNIE *(left)*
AND GREG DENNIE.

JEANNA HOUSTON, 48,

talks with her sister,

CONNOR BARNAS, 47

Jeanna Houston: We come from a long line of sisters who hated each other. [*Laughter.*] My grandmother and her sister hated each other, and then my mom and her sister did not get along. You and I used to have some pretty horrific fights, where I would say things that were just really inappropriate. But we broke the cycle. We were just like, *This isn't going to go on anymore.* And we stuck to it. I remember hugging you and telling you I loved you and that I never wanted to fight again. And I think that's when we became each other's support, best friend, and go-to person for everything.

I remember such sweetness in our relationship. One time we were coming in the back door and Dad said, "You girls complement each other." And you said to me, "Nice shirt!"

And I said, "Yeah, nice pants—" And he goes, "No, no, no. What I mean is, you each have characteristics that fit each other."

Connor Barnas: We were so different that we really were complementary. You would always get hurt so easily, so I would want to be in front of you, because things didn't hurt me. I always felt like your protector.

Jeanna: I am a year older, but I never felt like the big sister. You were stronger and more assertive—always poking and looking and discovering and adventuring. You were always teaching me things, and so it was like you were *my* big sister.

I was kind of in a shell for a lot of my life, and I think what caused me to go into a little bit of that shell was our older brother Nick's death when I was three—it set me up for a lifelong battle with depression. He was five years old when he had three unexplained seizures and eventually died.

Connor: When Nick died everything just kind of got shuffled. Before Nick's death, all the pictures that you would see of Daddy would be smiling and laughing, and then after, his whole demeanor was different.

Jeanna: What later came out was that when Nick passed, Dad felt responsible. But he kept that inside for over twenty years. So there was a lot of pain, and guilt, and shame. But somehow we were still able to be a happy family.

Connor: Yeah, I mean when I think about our home on Oriental Gardens Road, there was always a sense of wonder, and that anything could happen. I remember when we built that raft of hyacinth down in the ravine behind our house— there was just a freedom to what we did. And there's nothing bittersweet about those memories. As tragic as Nick's death was, and as dysfunctional as our family could be, there was absolutely a foundation of unconditional love. That was never a question.

I moved to New York when I was twenty, and I was partying a lot. I've always been a *push harder, faster, farther* person, and I just want to go and do and be and see—and so that's what I did. I started using drugs heavily. My goal was to be a working artist, but my idea of an artist was to be a suffering drug addict. And I look back on the years of being strung out on heroin and it was awful—terrible. And everybody thought I was going to die.

Jeanna: You almost did.

Connor: A couple times . . . But one of the greatest memories of my life is that when you married David and you guys got your own apartment, you said, "We have to get a two-bedroom so that when Connor wants to come home and change her life, she has someplace to come." And that so much symbolizes the profound openness and love that you have for me. So I moved to Jacksonville, and you had this whole life set up for me. I still saw you as my need-to-be-protected sister, but then the roles reversed because you were able to provide me with a safe haven, and I cleaned up.

Within four years, I was a radically different person.

Jeanna: But I was still suffering with depression, and I also started using drugs. Then I came to a point where I just realized the drugs weren't working—and so I followed you once again. That was thirteen years ago.

You are the grounding force in my life. I can call you on the phone and feel safe—and just love beyond imagination, friendship, joy, and a lot of laughter.

Connor: Today we have these really rich lives, and my son and your daughter are as in love with each other as you and I were. You always say *now* are the good old days. This is our dream come true.

RECORDED IN JACKSONVILLE, FLORIDA, ON NOVEMBER 2, 2012.

JEANNA HOUSTON *(left)*
AND CONNOR BARNAS.

DIANE HARTMAN, 52,

talks with her sister

KATHY HENRICKSON, 54

Diane Hartman: What do you remember about that little house we grew up in?

Kathy Henrickson: We were at the very edge of the desert, on the edge of nowhere. Mom always liked to tell us that when Dad brought her there the first time, she said it would do just fine but she couldn't imagine raising a family by the railroad tracks and the deep canal. Of course, we know that she raised us there and never left the place.

I remember very crowded quarters and lots of squabbling and noise—there were six of us, all in a ten-year span—and one bedroom for two parents and the kids. There was a closet that our sister could dress in because she was older and it was the only private place. Mom and Dad slept on the porch, which just had plastic over the windows in the winter and little bits of snow came blowing in.

Diane: Mom was a schoolteacher. She taught for several years before she had our oldest brother, Chuck, and then she didn't teach for eighteen years other than substituting. She had a two-year degree and by the time she wanted to go back, it required a four-year degree, so she went back to school. I can remember her sitting at that little kitchen table, studying with all this chaos going on around her. Do you remember that? Driving into Boise to go to school at night . . .

Kathy: I remember she would be gone to school for long days in the summer, and us kids were on our own. We would just fight and play. About an hour before she was ready to come home, we'd look at the clock, and then we'd hurry up and do all the things we were supposed to be doing all day. I also remember a few times being taken along to school and waiting for her in the car that she'd park in the shade.

Diane: When I was in the sixth grade, Mom saw an ad in the paper for a house for ten thousand dollars. She went to the bank, and then she went to see the house. I think it was a se-

cret until she had her ducks in a row. I remember it ha[...]
bedrooms and French doors. It was the fanciest thing.

Kathy: Yeah, that was a big, big change in our lives. [...]
some of us had to share rooms, and Mom and Dad had a [...]
bedroom. And don't forget the bathroom! [*Laughter.*] T[...]
home was our mother's castle. I think it really changed w[...]
we became. I was no longer ashamed to invite friends ove[...]
And I had some privacy, even though we did share a room[.]
Whose side was neat?

Diane: That would have been your side.

Kathy: And whose side was creative?

Diane: Oh, me! [*Laughs.*] That's very kind of you. But we
lost that house when it burned down on November 1, 2001.

Kathy: Early that morning, the phone rang and it was our
pastor's wife. She said, "Your parents' home is on fire. Your
dad is okay, but they're looking for your mom." So I ran to
get my husband and we got going. I could see the plume of
smoke when we were fifteen miles away.

When we got there, the neighbors had gathered as country folk do when there's a tragedy. The roads were lined.
Small community, but it doesn't seem small when something
like that happens. We couldn't park very close, and so I remember getting out of the car, and I ran from the corner up
over the railroad tracks and was met by a police officer. He

seemed to recognize that he couldn't stop me, so he ran alongside of me, between me and the house, protecting me. In the midst of tragedy, there's also these blessings that you remember later.

As I reached the end of the lane, which was getting close to where the home was, I was met by a man who was totally black with red eyes. It was the pastor from our parents' little church that they'd gone to for all of their marriage and before. He had been the one to see the fire and to try to help get our mom out of the house. And he's the one that prevented me from going to see Mom. He walked me back up the lane to where they were working on our father, who had smoke inhalation. So he refocused me on Dad, which was also a real kindness at that point.

But it wasn't going to be okay until you got there. And then you came up over the railroad track—my calm, cool, and collected sister—and your head was looking back and forth, searching. I poked my head out of the ambulance and saw you coming, and Dad was in there with tears running through the soot on his face. I'd only seen him cry once, and it was at their fiftieth anniversary.

We were not accepting that Mom was gone, but I think all those around us had. We drove to Boise together, which was thirty minutes away, and all that way, we talked. And by the

time we got to Boise, I think we both accepted that she couldn't have survived.

Diane: When the doctor walked out of the emergency room and sat down with us, he told us that she was gone. I asked if we could see her, and he said we could. So we went back to this room where she was, and I remember just holding on to you.

Kathy: Through her teaching she had touched so many lives—generations in that small community. A community had lost her, and a church family had lost her, and the grandchildren had lost her. People would say to us, "She saved my life." Or, "We had something special." She just made everyone feel that way.

Diane: It was an amazing funeral. We had it in the church that had been built around the little schoolhouse where she had her first teaching job. It was standing room only. You spoke at the service, because I couldn't. And I just grasped on to the things you said—they've helped me very much.

Kathy: We were close prior to the fire and losing Mom. But since losing Mom—it's just like breathing, practically.

Diane: I've never *once* not known where your heart lay. I've never once not known that you loved me. It's just like that old saying: A breath of kindness blows the chaff away.

Kathy: I miss Mom most in the quiet of a moment. I know

God said, "I know you want to keep her. And I didn't send this fire, but I'm going to use it to take her home to be with me." I feel more sure about this now than I have in some days past. And I believe it still . . . even on the days when it doesn't help.

RECORDED IN BOISE, IDAHO, ON MAY 19, 2008.

KATHY HENRICKSON *(left)*
AND DIANE HARTMAN.

MARYANNA CLARKE, 57,

talks with her husband,

CHRIS CLARKE, 60,

and their daughter,

KATE CLARKE, 22

Maryanna Clarke: Chris and I had moved to Nashville to be in the music business. I wanted to be a mom, but having a child seemed kind of counterproductive to pursuing a career in music. And so because we didn't plan to have a child, we didn't have one. And then I started to be involved in theater.

Chris Clarke: So here we were, a childless couple—comfortable, active, self-centered, and out late at night going to cast parties. My sister, Barbie, a very determined and independent single parent, had asked, "If something happened to me, would you take care of Kate?" And we said what people say: "Of course we would." But just after Kate's sixth birthday, on Thanksgiving, Barbie was in a car accident.

Kate Clarke: Myself, my friend Kelly, and my dad, David, were all in the accident. Kelly and I were not hurt, and David had a bunch of broken ribs and a broken collarbone. But it was fatal for my mom.

Before the accident, David was not in my daily life—he didn't know I existed until I was around age three. When he did find out, he wanted to meet me, and my mom had invited him over to where we lived in Kentucky for Thanksgiving. But I didn't really know him at all.

Chris: And we were already Chris and Maryanna to you—we had dispensed with "uncle" and "aunt," it just got in the way—so when the horrible phone call came that said Barbie was killed, we went racing off to Kentucky and came home with you.

Maryanna: You *not* coming to live with us was never an option. It just wasn't.

Chris: We folded you right into our routine. You started coming to rehearsals and cast parties with us, and I can remember you singing "Sweeney Todd" in the bathtub at the top of your lungs: "Swing your razor high!" You hit the ground at such a speed, and you taught me that, happy or sad, you have to march on through life.

I remember one evening, less than a year after you'd come to live with us, you and I were home alone and we found a box of old videotapes. So we put a videotape in, and we watched what turned out to be you as a two-and-a-half-year-old Christmas angel, all fidgety in a church pageant. The next shot was in the church basement, and in the door comes Barbie carrying you. That was the first time you had seen an image like that since she had died. You said, "My mommy!" And the next thing was just buckets of tears. Holding back my own tears, I said, "Let's make sure that we always have this videotape so someday we can look at it again." Then, when Maryanna came home two hours later, you said, "You have to see this videotape of me and my mommy!" So it was a horrible, sad memory the first time, and two hours later it was a happy one. That was just a big lesson for me.

Kate: I feel like I was a pretty happy-go-lucky six-year-old, but I know there were many, many nights where I was lying in my bed crying, being very mad at God for wanting my mom more than I wanted my mom.

I know you guys have said that I didn't come with an instruction book when I came to live with you. What would be some advice you would give yourself if you could go back?

Maryanna: I remember my friend told me that when she was four, her mother died and she went to live with her grandmother. And she told me to give you whatever you needed at night, because nighttimes were always the hardest for her. Up until that moment, I can remember trying to make you sleep in your own bed, just sitting by you until you went to sleep, and then trying to get back to my own bed to sleep for the night. I had been trying to find something in my life that I could hang on to that was the same as it had been, so that everything wasn't all upside down. But after that, everything changed. If you needed me to lie down with you and hold you and stay with you all night, that's what I did. And if you needed to come crawl into our bed, that's what we did. [*Crying.*] So, if I had to give myself advice, it would be to know that sooner.

And that's how you and I instituted our traditional evening chitchats. In bed, we'd talk about what we did during the day or you'd talk about stuff that was bothering you, like a spelling test at school that you were worried about.

One night we got to talking about our mothers. My mother died when I was twenty-one, and I said that I didn't remember the last time I saw my mother—I was in college when she died, so I hadn't marked that last moment. I was trying not to let you know that I was crying, but my voice kind of broke. You said, "Mare, are you crying?" And without my asking for anything, you got up out of bed, walked into the bathroom, brought me back a glass of water, and you held my hand.

Kate: When I was nine or ten we decided you and Chris would adopt me, because you were my parents in every single way except legally—and, well, biologically. But my biological dad had to give up his rights for you to take me as your own. It was very hard for you to figure out how to ask him, and I could see your distress.

So I remember I sent him a letter. I wrote, "Maryanna and Chris want to adopt me. Is that okay?" A couple of days later, you were talking about it again, and I remember being like, "Oh, I sent him a letter." You both freaked out, and I'm pretty sure there was a phone call, warning him.

Chris: Oh, there was! I got through, "We didn't want you to know this way, but we have been talking about pursuing adopting Kate . . ." And this is the most noble thing: he said, "If that's what Kate wants to do, that's what we should do." And so he did sign the petitions, and you officially became our daughter.

Maryanna: The hardest thing about those first years had been not knowing whether or not you were permanent in our life. And so it wasn't until we were finally able to adopt you that I could breathe.

Kate: I think one of the challenges now is learning to stay close without our chitchats every night. I mean, I might be an ocean away for a while, but I know that you guys have always said, "We're going to live a street away from you wherever you go." So I guess it's always in my head that you'll be nearby.

Maryanna: I can remember people saying when you first

came to live with us, Kate, how lucky you were. I never understood that because I didn't feel like you were the lucky one. We were the lucky ones. It wasn't just the fact that now there was a child in our life—it's that we got to have this privilege of having *you* as our daughter. And I'm looking forward to seeing the family that we will grow to become.

Chris: I always say: Our family started with a tragedy, but everything else after that is a miracle.

RECORDED IN NASHVILLE, TENNESSEE, ON MAY 12, 2012.

JUSTIN CLIBURN, 30,

talks with his wife,

DEANNE CLIBURN, 26

Justin Cliburn: I joined the National Guard in April of 2001. I would love to say that there were great patriotic reasons, but I was a senior in high school and I had no plan for college, so I joined for free college tuition. The day after I joined, a friend of mine said, "Are you crazy? If we go to war, you're the first to go." I remember telling him, "Yeah, but what are the chances of that happening?"

In December 2005, I found myself in Iraq. The entire year was a very surreal experience, and when I look back on things now, I understand just how terrifying that situation was.

Deanne Cliburn: Do you feel comfortable talking about Ali and Ahmed?

Justin: Yeah . . . I was at the police headquarters in north

Baghdad and saw this really filthy child walking through the compound with a large sack slung over his back, almost like Santa Claus. We tried to get his attention, but he was very shy and he didn't want to talk to us. For most of the soldiers, what really made our day was being able to give toys or candy to the children. And the children knew that, so a lot of them would congregate and hope to receive something. But this was the first kid that did not want to speak with us or be around us. He left that day, but he came back.

Through an interpreter, we learned that his name was Ali. He seemed about thirteen or fourteen, and he was there collecting cans for money. He lived in a very large slum on Baghdad's north side, and that was all he could do to help his family. I saw him collecting cans every day we were at that police station, and I would collect my cans during the week to give to him. The second or third time I met him, he brought his best friend, Ahmed. Ahmed was a little bit younger and much more outgoing. But with me, Ali also began to open up. Pretty soon we had this special relationship—we were about as close as people who don't speak the same language can be.

We would play rock, paper, scissors and kick around a soccer ball. They were just children, and they were happy to see us every day. I could speak or play with these kids and forget that I was in the middle of a war zone. Ali and Ahmed were like an oasis of innocence in this state of chaos.

It wasn't long before I realized that I wasn't going to change a thing in Baghdad, but I could try to change the life of these two kids. And so they became my life while I was there.

It was July 2006, I believe, when Ali showed up one day, and I could tell something wasn't right. He said, "Ahmed! Ahmed boom!" I got our interpreter, and he said Ahmed and his mother had gone to the gas station, and as they were leaving a suicide bomber detonated. Ahmed's mother died instantly. And Ahmed was in a hospital somewhere.

I remembered that the hospitals in Iraq needed money up front. And so other soldiers and I collected what cash we had and gave it to Ali and said, "Go take this to Ahmed's father." A few days later, I saw Ali walking up very slowly. He came to me and he sat down on the curb next to my Humvee, and he dug a hole in the ground with his fingers. Then he picked up a rock and said, "Ahmed," and put it in the hole. He put the dirt back over it, pointed to the ground, and said, "Ahmed." I sat on the curb with him, and we both cried.

The day that he told me Ahmed was dead was without a doubt the worst day of my life and still is. This was the first time I felt like I loved someone who wasn't my family member. I had never been in love at that point, and I didn't have any children. But it was almost as if I'd adopted a child, and as soon as I felt like this child really was mine, he was taken away.

But it was war, and we still had a mission every day. So I would wake up and I would do my job. I had six months left in Baghdad. And when I told Ali it was my last day, he burst into tears. I tried to console him, but he just kind of gave me a half hug and ran away. That was the last I saw him.

Deanne: Do you remember telling me about that for the first time?

Justin: We had not been dating very long. It was after *Gran Torino,* the Clint Eastwood film. In the end, essentially, Clint Eastwood dies to save the life of a child. I had the biggest pit in my stomach, and I knew that if I tried to speak, I was going to break down. I remember you asked, "What is it?" because you knew something was wrong. And then I remember saying, "He saved the child. And I couldn't save Ahmed." And that's when I really lost it.

Deanne: I could tell that you didn't want me to see that. You had pictures of both the kids in your house, and I always knew who they were, so I knew some of the story. But it wasn't until that night that I realized how incredibly close you were to them.

Justin: That wasn't the first time that I started to feel like I was going to break down, but it was the first time that somebody didn't change the subject as soon as they possibly could or leave the room or pretend they didn't notice. And you didn't leave that night.

You were still by my side when you realized the man you started dating wasn't all right. And you didn't waver. You said you'd always be there to hold me and listen to my stories. Because that pit . . . it's always there.

You're the first person I was really, truly in love with. And I still have this fear in the back of my mind: *What if the person I love is taken from me again?* Before you, the only people I loved that weren't my family were these children that I lost: Ahmed died, and I never saw Ali again. I don't even know what came of him, or if he was killed.

I really wish I was able to keep in touch, but that's the nature of war, I suppose—you meet people that you can't take home. But whenever I see footage from Baghdad, I'm always wondering if he's in the frame.

RECORDED IN NORMAN, OKLAHOMA, ON JUNE 27, 2012.

BETSY BROOKS, 52,

talks to her boyfriend,

JOHN GRECSEK, 47

Betsy Brooks: My father was a perfectionist. His favorite tool was his level. He was meticulous about the way he looked, he was meticulous about the house, the yard—everything. And he was a proud marine—I always say, we learned "The Marines' Hymn" before we knew our A-B-C's. But I was just cut from a different cloth. I think I was the bane of his tidy existence.

In the early days my father would always go back to work after dinner, and my mother was left home to babysit my sister and me. I had a big sense of adventure and a lot of energy, and my mother would make these lists of the things I did wrong during the day—all my day's crimes—and save them for my father when he came home from work. And he would turn positively livid. I grew very afraid of him, and we butted heads from the moment we could.

I think I moved out just about the day I turned eighteen. And my father came home from work early that day to make sure I didn't mess up the walls when I moved my bedroom furniture.

But after he retired, it started to become obvious that he wasn't himself. I remember one time I asked him to make some picture frames for me, because he loved to do that sort of stuff. But my mother called me up and she said, "Please, do me a favor and don't ask him to make them anymore. He had such a hard time."

After he was officially diagnosed with Alzheimer's, he became difficult for my mother to live with. He caused a lot of commotion in the house, and he would demand things over and over and over again. I guess he was looking for an ally, and he knew that if he had every single drawer out of the dresser or on the floor, I couldn't care less. So he turned to me.

I had wanted to please him all my life, and it seemed like I never could. And then all of a sudden, he just bonded to me. He became so easy to talk to. We would sit on the back porch and eat pistachio nuts and share a beer. My father was interested in everything. He was interested in flowers, and the neighbors, and my car, and my friends. I could tell him my secrets—it was just a beautiful thing. I got to enjoy all the good that was in him.

I loved my father tremendously. In the years since he got sick, we were so close and I enjoyed him so much—I wouldn't trade those eleven years for anything. Except I wish the price to pay for them wasn't so high.

RECORDED IN NEW YORK, NEW YORK, ON AUGUST 26, 2008.

MARCELA GAVIRIA, 43,

talks with her longtime doctor,

DEMPSEY SPRINGFIELD, 67

Marcela Gaviria: I had a rare cancer in 1976; I was seven years old. It was an era when I think only fifteen percent of the kids were making it through this illness.

Dempsey Springfield: You had a malignant tumor called a Ewing's sarcoma, and eventually you came to the University of Florida for a bone transplant. The treatment for the kind of tumor you had has changed dramatically, but when I started, we mainly did amputations and most patients didn't survive.

Marcela: When you're twelve, it's not like you're thinking about what your life will be like later on, but you do sense that a limb is a big thing to lose. You have all these dreams of going to the prom, and walking down the aisle, so you want to do anything you can to save your leg. And it mattered a lot to me that you would try to save it.

You'd walk in every morning with such a big smile, and you wore your bow ties—you just looked like a Southern gentleman. You were so warm and gentle, and you explained what was happening. You had a great bedside manner. If you had been a doctor-in-a-hurry, I think it would've made those months in the hospital just miserable. I survived partly because you were so kind.

Later on, I went to you every time I needed surgery. Maybe five years would go by and you'd have to redo something.

Dempsey: The strange thing is, in some ways, I keep moving and you keep following.

There would be a long period of time when I didn't hear from you or see you. Then you'd show up, and then be gone again. You've contacted me at three in the morning after not hearing from you in years.

I'm always nervous that I'm going to have to do something or tell somebody something that would be more difficult if I was too friendly, so I've always felt a little uncomfortable getting too close to patients. But you are different. And I don't have anywhere near as close a relationship with any other patient.

Marcela: I always wanted definitives, and you were really frank about what would happen next, as best you knew it. I appreciated it. I think I've always lived my life with a belief that if you're prepared for the worst, you can accept whatever outcome. So I just left those rose-colored glasses somewhere on the night table and never put them on.

I'd hate to count the amount of times you've operated on me, but I always wanted to get better for you. When you're sick in bed and you don't have a lot to look forward to, looking forward to seeing your doctor the next day and giving him an update sort of propels you to health.

You actually said something to me that I have always held very dear. You said, "You will be amazed at how the human spirit adapts to anything." And I think you're so right. We all have our problems; it's just that some are evident—like mine. When I walk down the street, I walk with a cane. And if I happen to be wearing a bathing suit at the beach, you would notice that my leg's been through a lot. But I feel proud of myself. I feel like a warrior: I've been through battles, but I'm on the other side. And I owe every scar on my leg to you.

It's funny. I would complain all the time about how I'd never get married, because I always wondered how difficult it would be for someone to sign up to my life. They have to know that my leg may be missing one day, and that there will be a lot of tough hospitalizations. But the fairy tale did actually happen, because I got married about two months ago— June 23 of this year. And I wanted you to have the first dance.

It was a way of celebrating that a lot of what I'm able to do nowadays is because of you.

Dempsey: Well, I was very happy to do it. I'd never been to a patient's wedding, and it *was* kind of out of a storybook. You came down the aisle with your mother. And everybody was so happy to be there.

Marcela: I am a bit of a walking miracle: I ride my bicycle and I go to the gym; I go up mountains, I go down mountains. And it's because I had the opportunity to have a great surgeon that really cared to get it right.

RECORDED IN BROOKLINE, MASSACHUSETTS, ON SEPTEMBER 14, 2012.

TIM OWENS, 54,

talks with his friend
BARBARA SCHUYLER, 75

Tim Owens: I was born in El Paso, Texas, to a military family. My father was a military policeman and an alcoholic, and my mother was a stay-at-home wife who was a drug addict and an alcoholic. I recall one time when I got sent home with a note pinned to my shirt that I did not know my multiplication tables. My mother read the note, kept me home from school the next day, and informed me that I would learn to multiply from one to nine before my father got home or she would personally teach me.

I spent the day frantically trying to learn. My mother called me into the kitchen, made me remove my clothing, and screamed, "What are six eights?" I was unable to answer, so she took my father's heavy, black leather gun belt and said,

"Timothy, I'm going to teach you what six times eight is. I'm going to hit you and when I stop, you count and you'll know what six times eight is." I was barely conscious by forty-eight.

I knew eventually one of us was going to die and it was not going to be her. So I ran away from home when I was fifteen. I spent my next five years on the street, living from empty restroom to empty restroom, and getting into men's cars, going to their homes, and having sex with them just for a place to sleep. Statistically, I shouldn't even be here—I should be on the back of a milk carton or buried in a shallow grave.

Later, I got a job as an assistant in a nursing home, and I became quite close with a gentleman I took care of. He informed his wife that when he died he didn't care if he was buried in a sheet just so he could pay for me to go to nursing school. And so his wife honored his request, and I became a licensed practical nurse. That was my journey to sanity and to fullness of life.

Some eighteen years ago, I found myself caring for a college professor in Louisville, Kentucky, who was quadriplegic. And you, his wife, were busy running the home and managing him.

Barbara Schuyler: I could tell whether a nurse was going to be good as soon as I opened the door, and you passed the test. You were an *outstanding* nurse. Part of your job was to teach as well as to take care of the patient yourself, and you were excellent. And the caregiving and blessings have been two ways.

Tim: You had gone to Seattle for the birth of your first grandchild, so I stayed with Bill. I had what I thought was the flu—I just didn't feel good—but I couldn't leave Bill. Then a little bit of fever got to be more of a fever, and I remember going into the bathroom and just lying on the cool tile because I was so hot. When you came home, I weighed about a hundred thirty pounds. You said, "What's wrong?" And I said, "I have AIDS." I went and had the test, and sure enough . . . I came home, and I remember you all crying.

When y'all retired to Seattle, you said, "We're not going to leave you here to do this alone. We're going to help you— you're coming with us." And so I came to Seattle, where you've spoon-fed me six times a day and watched over me constantly.

I think of all the times that I worked hard to make sure that a patient was comfortable and well taken care of, and now it's completely reversed—you're here for me.

Barbara: Well, you were there for us at the end of Bill's life. I asked the doctor to wait until you got there to explain his condition, and I was really grateful and happy you were there at that moment when I was making one of the most difficult decisions I ever made.

Tim: You have become my family and my world, and I've gotten so much more from you than I ever gave. Y'all have taught me how to love art, how to love books, how to love music and good food—and how to live. I don't survive anymore; I live a full and complete life. I'm very, very blessed, and it is all because I came to you one day for an interview as a nurse. I never knew what I was going to walk away with.

The horrid way I was treated as a child and living on the street, trying to survive, has all been washed away. I have a family: I had your husband, my father, Bill, and I have you, Barbara, my mother. Not many people get to choose a family, but I've been fortunate enough to be able to choose mine.

RECORDED IN SEATTLE, WASHINGTON, ON FEBRUARY 16, 2012.

This interview was a part of the StoryCorps Legacy Initiative for people in hospice care or otherwise facing serious illness.

GWENEVIERE MANN, 40,

talks with her boyfriend,

YASIR SALEM, 34

Gweneviere Mann: I woke up one morning in mid-November of 2008 and I was almost completely blind in my left eye. I went to the eye doctor, who said I should see a neurologist immediately and get an MRI done. It was found that I had a large tumor resting on my optic nerve, so I went in for surgery seven days later.

Yasir Salem: I was actually relieved, because we thought everything would go back to normal after you got your surgery.

Gweneviere: But as a result of the work that it took to get the tumor out, I suffered a stroke, and I now have short-term memory loss. The doctors say the brain can continue healing up to two years, but whatever is not back by that point is not likely to ever come back . . . And I'm more than two years out from my brain surgery. So the fact is, I'm going to have to live the rest of my life this way.

Yasir: Is it frightening to lose your memory?

Gweneviere: It's very frightening. And the thing that scares me the most is the thought that I will wake up one day and I'll be eighty years old and I won't remember the last forty years of my life.

It used to be so effortless to remember things. Now remembering for me is sort of like trying to remember a dream you had a few nights ago—I can only hold on to things for maybe an hour or so. So I have to write down when I eat meals. Sometimes I might eat lunch three times because I don't remember that I ate already. And I always have a note card in my pocket that tells me what the date is.

One of the big problems I have is feeling connected with people in my life. It could be that I'm seeing my friends and talking to my family on a regular basis, but because I have no memory of it, it's as if it doesn't happen. So it's become really important to me to keep a journal and take lots of photographs. That way I can see that I'm not totally alone. And you've helped me so much—you've been wonderful throughout this experience.

Yasir: Do you remember some of the funny stories—

well, they're funny now—about when you first came out of surgery?

Gweneviere: Well, I know that I used to always think I was in San Francisco, and you would say, "We're not in San Francisco! Look out the window!"

Yasir: What are those things called? Do you remember?

Gweneviere: Yeah, confabulations. Do you remember another funny confabulation that I used to have?

Yasir: You used to think that your coworker Barbara was your mom, even though she's a completely different race than you.

Gweneviere: Oh, that's right!

Yasir: And there was one point when you were confused because you thought we had broken up. And I would ask you, "Why do you think you're staying at my place?" And you're like, "Well, we're just cool like that."

Gweneviere: [*Laughs.*] Sorry about that.

Yasir: Thankfully, you got over that. Is there anything positive that has come out of losing your memory?

Gweneviere: I ran the New York City Marathon with you, my boyfriend. That was a really big deal to me. And one of the things that I asked you to do to help me, as a trick, was to not let me look at any of the mile markers along the way. And if I asked you how long we'd been running, to always tell me "ten or fifteen minutes." It worked like a charm! As we were running across the finish line, you said to me, "Here come the waterworks," because I always cry out of happiness. And I started crying my eyes out. [*Laughs.*]

You've been there for me more than I could ever have asked. You have been my rock—my one real, stable thing.

RECORDED IN NEW YORK, NEW YORK, ON FEBRUARY 12, 2011.

SADIE GILMORE MARION-LONG,

60, talks with her longtime friend and housemate, JANICE BLACK, 59

Sadie Gilmore Marion-Long: You lived in the J. H. Gunn neighborhood, in Charlotte, with your father, your step-mother, and your stepsister, and I used to come to you all's house. Everybody thought you were dumb, so they thought I was there for your stepsister, Betty. But you and I formed our own friendship.

Your mama died when you was nine years old, and then after your father was deceased, you ended up living in the house with just your step-people. It really didn't look good to me. You were just the maid for everybody: You would take care of your stepsister's five children. You did the cleaning. You took the garbage out. You did ninety-five percent of the work that was done inside, and everybody would just walk past you. At four and a half feet tall, we couldn't see you for all the clothes in your arms.

When I seen you doing these type of things, and all these people were sitting around doing nothing, that really shook me up. Nobody paid you no attention. But I couldn't just walk away.

So when your stepmother allowed us to go out together, she said, "You're going to have to watch her—Janice will walk off." And that was a little disturbing, because there ain't but four streets in the little community where we live. Everybody knew everybody.

And so we went 'cross the railroad tracks, about three blocks from where you lived. I said, "Janice, Miss Carrie told me to watch you, because you might walk off." And you said, "Where the hell am I going to walk off to? There ain't but a couple streets down here, and they won't let me go nowhere." So I thought, *Oh Lord, she ain't dumb at all. She got plenty of sense.*

From that point, we started talking about everything and everybody. I just let you be Janice. I just let you feel free as a bird to flap your wings. But I could see the expression on your face when I would take you back. You just looked so sad.

Janice Black: I got tired of taking care of other people's kids and being a maid. I didn't have a life. I had to get out, and you helped me.

Sadie: You would come over to my house and visit on the weekends, and one day I was in the room when you was changing clothes, and I said, "What in the world happened to you?"

Janice: I told you they had me sign a paper and the next thing I knew, I was in the hospital—and they didn't tell me what I was in there for.

Sadie: One night, I'd seen on TV about the North Carolina sterilizations. So when you got up the next morning to go to work, I told you what I had seen, and I asked, "Janice, do you want me to see if you're one of those victims?" And you said yes. So I called, and it took about six to eight weeks for me to get the findings back. The package came with all the paperwork pertaining to the sterilization, who signed it—everything. The whole nine yards.

Janice: They had me fixed.

Sadie: You have to give a reason that you want a family member sterilized. Your stepmother said they were afraid you were going to get pregnant, because you would leave the house and she wouldn't know you were gone. But you never went anywhere. That made me really, really upset. I had to stop reading.

I don't have no Ph.D.'s behind my name, but I do know right from wrong. And so do you. And they did you wrong. They didn't even give you an opportunity to have a child.

Janice: They didn't give me a chance.

Sadie: But you know what? Look at the five babies you did raise—your stepsister's kids. You can always say when you see them: "I raised her from a baby. I took care of her. I wiped her nose. I cleaned her bottom. I fixed her bottle." And most important: You rocked them to sleep. And when nobody else was there for them to look at when they woke up, who was there?

Janice: I was.

Sadie: That's right. You have worked real hard. You really, really have.

I thank God for you. He gave you me because he knew that we had unconditional love between us. You know a lot of things that I don't know and vice versa. So put what we got together, and we think we're the smartest two gals on this green earth, don't we?

Janice: We know we is.

Sadie: You know, sometimes families don't have to be the families that your mama and daddy had. You can find friends that are a better family to you than your own. So although we're not biologically tied, we are spiritually tied.

Janice: Your house is the White House to me. In my book, it's the White House!

Sadie: Sometimes, when you leave out in the morning and you hug me so tight, you're about to squeeze the breath out of me. I say, *Lord, she needs to turn me loose, because I can't breathe!* But you know what? It's the way you hug me in the mornings that lets me know. It makes me feel real special.

Janice: We're friends to the end. And that will never change.

Sadie: Friends till we're graveyard dead. And I love you with all my heart.

Janice: Sadie, I love you too.

RECORDED IN CHARLOTTE, NORTH CAROLINA, ON MARCH 22, 2012.

Beginning in 1933, the Eugenics Board of North Carolina sterilized an estimated 7,600 men, women, and children whom they deemed slow or mentally ill. In the 1950s and '60s the program increasingly targeted African American women. The North Carolina Eugenics program ended in the 1970s.

SADIE GILMORE
MARION-LONG *(left)*
AND JANICE BLACK.

BRYAN WILMOTH, 46,

talks with his brother

MIKE WILMOTH, 42

Bryan Wilmoth: I never really told Mom and Dad that I was gay, but Dad used to go through our stuff, I guess, and he found a love letter from a guy buried in my box of things. I was probably nineteen by then, and I kept that letter with me because it was the first love note I ever got. Dad read this letter and lost it. So he took me for a ride and dropped me off in the country in the middle of the night with a five-dollar bill. All I remember is sleeping outside.

I really missed my brothers and sisters when I left. I remember hearing that if I called the house and you guys talked to me that you'd get a beating, because Dad didn't want you to "catch gay." So I wouldn't call. I knew Mom and Dad were talking about how horrible gay people were and how I was probably going to hell—and you guys believed that.

So as each of you guys moved out or got kicked out of the house—or, in your case, ran away at thirteen and a half—I would make an effort to contact you and try to be a big brother again. At first, you were really resistant. And it took a long time for our relationship to build. You didn't know anything about gay people—

Mike Wilmoth: Didn't want to. Granted, it was fear based.

Bryan: Of course. But it was still something I had to try to fix. I remember after you started to accept it, every time you met another gay person you would say, "You've got to meet my brother!" [*Laughs.*] I always thought that was really funny, and really sweet.

Mike: Do you remember when you found out that you were HIV positive?

Bryan: It was 1985, and I was twenty-three. They told me I had six to eighteen months to live. When I called Dad and told him I was HIV positive, he said, "Boy, you'll do anything for attention, won't you?" At first I was really shocked. But I think it was actually the best thing he could've said, because I was going to need a lot of emotional support, and right up front I knew that that wasn't where I was going to get it.

Dad wanted nothing to do with Mom's side of the family,

and so we had been estranged from Granny and Grandpa. And then I got a message from our aunt Kathy, who I hadn't talked to in years. She said, "I know it's short notice, but Granny and Grandpa are having their fiftieth wedding anniversary day after tomorrow, and I just thought somebody from your family should know." I mean, this is my mom's parents, and Mom's got eight kids and nobody knew that Granny and Grandpa were having their fiftieth wedding anniversary. So I called Kathy back and I got on a Greyhound that night.

I remember walking in with Aunt Kathy, and Granny and Grandpa were sitting at the head table with this huge banner over them that said "50 Years." Way across the room, Grandpa Guy stood up and said, "Is that Bryan?" And he came all the way around, grabbed my arm, and gave me a big hug. He took me up to the front table and put me right next to him and Granny.

We talked the whole night long. They already knew that I was gay and they knew I was HIV positive, but Grandpa wanted to know everything. He wanted to know if I'd ever been in love, he wanted to know if I was happy . . . I never expected to have a night like that with my grandpa.

Mike: That event opened the doors for all of us with Mom's side of the family.

Bryan: That's true, isn't it? After that, I started telling you guys what great people they were, and that's when we started coming back together as brothers and sisters: Bryan, Pam, Chris, Mike, Jude, Amy, Josh, and Luke-Henry.

Now, Luke-Henry I didn't even know because he wasn't born till I was nineteen or twenty. I hadn't seen him—ever— and he never got to talk to me. But when he graduated from high school, he called me and said, "Bryan? This is your little brother Luke." And I lost it.

He was estranged from Mom and Dad, too, and he was about to go to University of Dallas. So I took my savings, which wasn't a lot, and I bought a round-trip ticket to Dallas. Mind you, this is a white-bread Catholic Christian school, and I'm the big gay brother running around getting him set up for his dorm room.

At one point I think I said to Luke, "I really feel more like a parent than a big brother." And he just looked at me, and he said, "You know, I really needed a parent this weekend." He was that kind of kid. So we go through this whole weekend, and the last event is this huge mass. I sat in the church, and after the ceremony, this bell rang and all the kids said good-bye to their parents and started heading down towards the dorms. I gave Luke a hug and a kiss and told him how much I loved him, and he started walking away. He got way down to the bottom of the hill and I was just watching after him, like, *Wow, I finally got to be a big brother.* And at that moment, he turned around and mouthed, "I love you." It was the most beautiful moment I had ever experienced. That changed everything for me.

Mike: You brought eight siblings that were so far apart as close together as we all became. You are my mountain.

Bryan: Even though Dad didn't treat me well, and to this day doesn't speak to any of his eight children, I still love him very much. Because if it hadn't been for him, I never would've found myself living the life that I'm living today.

I just want to tell you that whenever I think of doing something with the person closest to me, I always think of you, because there's nobody else I've ever felt safer with, Mike. I even moved in with you when I got sick. And I want you to know how much it means to me that you've loved me like this. For that I will be forever grateful. It is the foundation relationship that I've put the rest of my life on.

RECORDED IN LOS ANGELES, CALIFORNIA, ON FEBRUARY 15, 2009.

MIKE WILMOTH *(left)*
AND BRYAN WILMOTH.

"Two Sides of the Same Heart"

MARY JOHNSON, 58,

talks with

OSHEA ISRAEL, 34

*In 1993, Oshea Israel, 16, got into an argument with
Laramiun Byrd, 20, at a party, and he shot and killed him.
Laramiun was Mary Johnson's only son.*

Mary Johnson: You took my son Laramiun's life, and I needed
to know why.

The first time I asked you to meet with me, you said,
"Absolutely not." So I waited nine months and asked you
again—and you said yes. You and I finally met in March 2005
at Stillwater Prison. I wanted to know if you were in the same
mind-set of what I remembered from court when you were
sixteen. But you were not that sixteen-year-old boy anymore.
You were a man. You entered, and we shook hands. I just told
you that I didn't know you; you didn't know me. You didn't

know my son; my son didn't know you. But we needed to get to know one another. And that's mainly what we did for two hours. We talked.

Oshea Israel: I found out that your son's and my life paralleled. We had been through some of the same things, and somehow we got crossed. And I took his life—without even knowing him. But when I met you, he became human to me.

When it was time to go, you broke down and started shedding tears. And then you just started going down, and the initial thing I tried to do was just hold you up in my arms. I'm thinking, *I can't let her hit the ground.* So I just hugged you like I would my own mother.

Mary: After you left, I said, "I just hugged the man who murdered my son." And that's when I began to feel this movement in my feet. It moved up my legs and it just moved up my body. When I felt it leave me, I instantly knew that all that anger and hatred and animosity I had in my heart for you for twelve years was over. I had totally forgiven you.

Oshea: Being incarcerated for so long, you tend to get detached from real love from people. Sometimes I still don't know how to take receiving forgiveness from you. How do you forgive someone who has taken your only child's life? To know that I robbed you of that, and for you to forgive me . . . you can't really put it into words.

I served seventeen years of my twenty-five-year sentence,

and since I got out, I see you almost every day. Although I can never replace what was taken from you—I can never fill that void—I can do the best that I can to be right there for you. I didn't want you to wonder what this guy was doing since he got out of prison. And now, you can actually *see* what I'm doing—you live right next door.

Mary: It's amazing. We have our conversations on our porch, and we share our stories—

Oshea: They go from "Hey, I found a job opportunity for you" to "Boy, how come you ain't called over here to check on me in a couple days? You ain't even asked me if I need my garbage to go out!" [*Laughter.*] I find those things funny, and I appreciate it all. I admire you for your being brave enough to offer forgiveness, and for being brave enough to take that step. It motivates me to make sure that I stay on the right path.

Mary: I know it is not an easy thing to talk about, us sitting here, looking at each other right now. So I admire that you can do this.

Oshea: Regardless of how much you see me stumble out here, you still believe in me. You still have the confidence that I'm going to do the right thing, and you still tell me to keep moving forward, no matter what.

Mary: You know, I didn't see Laramiun graduate, but you're going to college, and I'll be able to see you graduate.

I didn't see him get married. But hopefully, one day I'll be able to experience that with you. Our relationship is beyond belief.

Oshea: I agree. I love you, lady.

Mary: I love you too, son.

RECORDED IN MINNEAPOLIS, MINNESOTA, ON APRIL 18, 2011.

GEORGE ROBINSON, 62,

talks to his daughter

KATIE ROBINSON, 19

George Robinson: I was raised by an outstanding man. But as I was growing up, various relatives would leak to me that he was not my biological father, and so I always wondered about that.

In my mom's generation, you never talked about a birth out of wedlock—which I was. "You don't need to know" was always the response my mom gave me. But my aunts would give me bits of information. I heard that my biological father was in the service and he served in Fort Dix, New Jersey. I also heard that he was a sergeant in the army and his nickname was "Sarge." He worked in food service, and he would take food and give it to poor people in the community. That made me really want to get to know him.

Growing up, I knew that I was a little bit different. I carried an attaché case in grade school and high school. My grandmother and a couple of my uncles lived with us, and they all looked a little bit different than me.

Every year, I would get a physical with a doctor, and the form would always ask for information about the illnesses that your parents had. I knew diabetes ran rampant through my mother's family, but I could never tell anything about my father. I actually used to make stuff up; I was really embarrassed that I didn't know my biological father. Every year, I would think about him: What was he like? Was he a man of integrity? Was he a man of character?

Katie Robinson: So what led to your decision to make the first phone call?

George: I decided to do a search for Jesse Fulmore—at that time I knew his name. And three Jesse Fulmores came up. One in Maryland, one in Philadelphia, and one in Burlington, New Jersey. And two of them were about the same age that I anticipated my biological father to be. I picked the one in Philadelphia.

Katie: Just out of the blue?

George: Out of the blue. I dialed the number, and before it started ringing I was so emotional I had to hang up. I said, *What if this is his number? What if he's dead? He'd be about eighty-nine years old now.* But I said, *I'm going to call him anyway.* So I dialed again, and Ruby, his wife, answered the phone. And I said, "My name is George Robinson. If Mr. Fulmore is not alive, I'm really sorry to make this call. But if he is, I would love to ask you a couple of questions about him, because I think I might be related to him." She said, "Mr. Fulmore is eighty-nine-years old now. He's alive. And sure, you can ask me questions."

And so here were the questions I asked and the answers she gave me: I said, "Was Mr. Fulmore in the service during 1948, 1949, in Fort Dix, New Jersey?" And she said, "Yes." And then I said, "Was Mr. Fulmore employed in food service?" And she said, "Yes." And I said, "Was Mr. Fulmore's nickname Sarge?" And she said, "Yes." The answer to everything was yes.

I was getting real nervous as it was going on, and my heartbeat started rising, and I said to her, "I think I might be Mr. Fulmore's son, and he probably doesn't know about it. I'm not looking for anything. God has been good to me, and I have a beautiful family, and everything is great. I just need to complete this part of my life." She said, "Yes, no problem at all! He should be back in a few minutes."

And while that was going on, he came home, and I asked him the entire list of questions again. He said, "Young man, if you know this much about me, you must be my son. When are you coming to visit me?"

He went on to say, "I've got five daughters and one passed away. I've always wanted a son, and now I have one."

I stayed up most of the night in anticipation of how that meeting would go. I was wondering, *Should I really go?* But then I said, *Finally, after fifty-seven years, I have an opportunity to meet my biological father!* I said, *I'm going!* So I got on the plane and got there early Sunday afternoon.

Katie: So what was it like when you finally got to meet your father in person?

George: When I pulled up to the house, he was on the doorstep. And what was really funny, Katie—I had on a gray suit; he had on a gray suit. I had on a black cashmere overcoat; he had on a black cashmere overcoat. I had on a black top hat that I always wear, and he had on a black hat very similar to mine.

Tears were just flowing out of his eyes, and tears were flowing out of my eyes, and we embraced on the steps for about ten minutes. The first thing he did, after we initially introduced ourselves, was he put his hands on my face like he was trying to feel, *was I really him, his son?* And then he touched my head the same way and then touched each of my knees individually. And then he touched each of my legs and looked at my feet. And then he put his hands next to mine—almost to see if they were alike—and it was almost the same vein structure on both sides. He was just in awe.

I had the plan that I would be there four, five hours, and then I would leave. But I ended up spending three days with him. We talked about so many different things. He said, "I dated a beautiful lady for a short period of time, but I did not know anything about you. If so, I would have definitely stepped in and taken care of you." And I said, "Listen, I don't want to go back to any of that. In the time that we have, I want to know everything about you."

At that time, my mom was on her deathbed, in hospice care. And my father wanted to go visit her. I said, "No, my mom wouldn't want you to see her in this condition. But I don't think she's going to be here for very long, and when she passes, you're welcome to come to her funeral."

My mom did pass, and at the funeral, my dad came with his family. He gave everybody in the family a red rose to set on Mom's casket. And he sat right in back of me, and he had

his hand on my shoulder the entire service. With him being there, I felt that I lost one part of me and I found another.

RECORDED IN EDINA, MINNESOTA,
ON JUNE 8, 2011.

DIANE TELLS HIS NAME, 60,

talks with her daughter,

BONNIE BUCHANAN, 22

Diane Tells His Name: I grew up in Covina, California, in the 1950s and '60s. My mother did real estate and my father was a plumbing contractor, and on Saturday mornings I would go with him on all of his jobs—I was his hang-out guy, learning how to do plumbing and things. I had a lot of friends, and I was just kind of happy-go-lucky.

I had a younger sister, Reggie, who was born when I was about two and a half. I didn't like the same things that she did: She would do tea parties and play with dolls, and I was always outside, looking at the clouds or the stars. My parents called me their earth child. My sister grew up blond, hazel eyed, and tall and thin like my mother, and I was short, round, and brown. People were always saying, "Are you sure you're from that family?" But my parents said I was a "throwback"—meaning I looked Indian because there was Indian in the family two or three generations back. My father's mother was five-eighths Creek Indian.

I think like follows like—you look for someone who's similar to you—and I always went towards dark-skinned people. In college, I lived in the Escondido area near San Diego, and Indian people would always look at me and nod their head up and purse their lips towards me, like, *Hey.* I went back to college in my thirties, and I chose Native American studies as my major. I remember going to powwows, and thinking, *Gee, I'm just an Irish-German girl. Why am I even at this powwow?*

In 1984, Dad and I took a vacation through Utah, where we visited my aunt Grace. She pulled out some old photo albums, and I saw a picture of my mom in October of 1951. It shocked me because I was born in November of 1951, and my mother was not pregnant in the picture. So that's when my inklings that I may be adopted started to be solidified.

At the time, I worked for my mom and dad at their mini-market and I kept having arguments with my mother. One day, after a particularly difficult day with my mom, I called

my aunt Shirley—my mom's youngest sister—in Oklahoma.
I said, "Aunt Shirley, am I adopted?" And my aunt Shirley
didn't say anything. Then she said, "That's something you
need to talk to your parents about." So that's when I knew. I
was thirty-seven.

Bonnie Buchanan: How did you feel?

Diane: It was satisfying to know that I wasn't crazy. But I
wasn't angry with my folks. In the fifties and sixties, when I
was growing up, you just didn't talk about those things.

My mom said later that she wished they would've told
me I was adopted when I was younger, but my dad said that
he would've gone to his grave without me ever knowing.
He'd say, "You're my baby. Whatever your background was,
it didn't matter, because when you came to us, you were
ours." I appreciated that he was so fervent about that, and I
always refer to them as my mom and dad because they're the
ones who raised me.

Initially my mom and dad said that they would help me—
they started telling me as much as they knew, which wasn't
very much. But then they became pretty adamant that I
shouldn't be trying to find my birth mother. So I started
looking for her on my own, because I didn't want to hurt my
folks. But our relationship really deteriorated at that point.

In April of 1988, I was put in touch with a volunteer

worker, who did all the work to get my sealed adoption file open and get my original, unaltered birth certificate. And when I got my birth certificate, it said my birth mother's name—and that she was born at the Pine Ridge Indian Reservation.

Bonnie: How did you feel when you had found your mom?

Diane: My whole identity just flip-flopped. There was a whole family—a whole *culture*—that I'd not been privileged to know. It was unbelievable to see her name and to realize that this was really happening. So I wrote to her, and we made arrangements for her to come meet me and my family on Valentine's Day 1989.

We went to the airport to meet Bell, my birth mother, and as I saw her coming down the escalator, it was like this apparition of this person I knew I was blood connected to for generations and generations and generations. It was thrilling. She stayed with us for two weeks to get to know the family.

Grandma Bell was very adamant that I go to South Dakota to receive my Indian name and get introduced into the tribe—it was just a crash course in how to be an Indian. And when I heard the people speaking the Lakota language, I felt like those words should be coming from my mouth. I felt like they were in my head and my heart already. And later on Grandma Bell did tell me that she spoke to me the whole nine months mainly in Indian, and she would sing Indian lullabies to me.

When I turned forty, your dad and I told Indian Family Services we wanted to adopt from my tribe, preferably a Lakota child. And after eight months or so, they faxed us a picture of a cute little Indian child in a jumper who was drinking chocolate syrup, full tilt, out of a Hershey's bottle. Our son Kenrick said, "That's her! That's the one we need to adopt!" And it was you. You came to us in June of 1992, when you were two years old.

When you were about five, I started doing research on your family—your birth mother is from Cheyenne River, and your birth father is from Pine Ridge. And when I started looking at your family tree, I saw one of my relatives, so we're actually related. I thought that was just amazing.

Bonnie: It's been a great blessing to be in this family, and I'm so glad you adopted me. I hope that someday my kids will hear this story and feel the connection.

Diane: You know, my adoptive mom, Betty, passed away in '93. And eighteen months later, my dad passed away. And I see now where that left a door open, because for the past almost twenty years since my parents passed away, I've gotten to know my birth mother very, very well. And I'm so happy to have you and to have been able to raise you in the native culture. It's like our whole family was planned so that it would be the best for all of us.

RECORDED IN SAN FRANCISCO, CALIFORNIA, ON OCTOBER 11, 2012.

STARR COOKMAN, 37,

talks with her friend
KYLEE MORELAND FENTON, 37

Starr Cookman: I remember in Mr. Kent's class in the sixth grade, I zeroed in on you. I don't know what it was, but I really felt that you were part of my tribe. And it felt inevitable that we would have a connection, whether you knew it or not, so I just tenaciously stayed near you as we went through sixth grade, and we got closer and closer.

And then we made it official with our blood sister ceremony. The night before, we were huddled underneath my bed making big plans: We decided that we needed water involved, so we had planned it all around the wash in Tucson, which is a body of water that only runs after the monsoons. And because we saw our parents celebrate important things with alcohol, we decided that we needed to have alcohol involved—even though we were only eleven—so we stole a beer from my dad's fridge. And because we had been church-goers, we decided that ritual usually meant a bettering of someone's soul, and so we decided that we were going to be better people after this blood sister ritual. Do you remember what we said to each other? "No more swear words!"

And so the whole idea was, we were going to take a cactus needle, and I was going to prick your thumb, and you were going to prick my thumb. We were to smoosh our blood to-gether, and *voilà*! It was going to be set.

So we got out to the wash with our Coors beer and our plan. You pricked my finger, but when it was time for me to prick yours, I just couldn't do it, so you pricked your own finger. At that point we knew that you were going to be a nurse, because it was no problem for you. And then we got to say our favorite swear word for the last time, and made the pact that we'd hit each other if it came out again. Then we guzzled the beer, went over to the wash, and floated the empty Coors beer can on a piece of driftwood off into the distance. I knew for sure that even if circumstances took us apart from each other, we were truly connected at the heart for the rest of our lives.

Kylee Moreland Fenton: When you and I were youngsters we had some really big ideas about how we wanted to live our adult lives together. You had this idea that I'll never forget:

You said that people always choose family, that people move places and change careers for their spouses. And you said to me, "Why can't we do that for our friendship?"

So we went about deciding how we were going to make that work. We decided that we wanted our own careers and wanted our children raised by people that shared our values and ideals. I always had this vision in my mind that my angry child would someday storm out of my house and that she could go right out my back door and into your front door. She would find the comfort that I've always known from you, and I would know that I could one hundred percent trust whatever guidance you wanted to give her. So she could have you and your family as a backup. If you think about it, that was a pretty tall order for a couple of thirteen-year-olds.

Starr: We didn't get reinforcement for that idea—we got a lot of pats on the head and "Oh, that's a nice idea, girls, but life happens."

But look at where we are now: We're living right down the street from each other. You have been helping me raise my two kiddos for the past six years. One day every week they go to you. And I have your sweet twenty-month-old baby one day a week, too. We can keep our careers, and we can still be close to each other. And we've found men who understand and honor our friendship. So we're still connected at the hip twenty-six years later.

You were there during the delivery of my first child, Rowan. My husband and I brought him home, and he was beautiful and perfectly healthy and wonderful. But by about the eighth day, I noticed that he had been spitting up his feedings. I had read that babies spit up, you know, but I just didn't know what was happening. You're a labor and delivery nurse, and so I asked you to listen to Rowan.

Kylee: I remember just watching him breathe. I was counting his respirations, and I remember feeling very alarmed— he was breathing so fast. But he had no other symptoms.

Starr: You said, "I would call your pediatrician." So we brought him to the pediatrician, and by the time we got there his respirations were lower. The doctor took his pulses, and they seemed okay.

Kylee: I said, "I'm really concerned. Why would he just for no reason be breathing a hundred times a minute?"

Starr: So then the doctor says, and I'll never forget these words, "They're gonna think I'm crazy at the children's hospital, but I think you guys should go there and get a chest X-ray for Rowan." So we got him into the car and drove to Children's together.

Kylee: The resident checked him all out and said, "Everything seems just fine. Before we send you home, I'm just gonna have the attending in the ER come in and listen to him." The attending came in and listened to Rowan's heart with his stethoscope. And then he got up and he shut the door and he came back and he listened some more. And he listened some more, and he listened some more. And then he had Rowan get an EKG.

Starr: At that point I was looking at you like, *What are we doing up here in cardiology?* Then the doctor said, "Rowan has something wrong with his heart. And I think we're gonna need to do surgery as soon as possible." And he left the room.

I looked at you and the room was so dark. I feel like I fell apart. You called everybody that needed to be called to tell them that Rowan was not doing well. You knew instinctively what to do and you stepped up to the plate. You really took over where I couldn't.

He was in heart failure at that point, and we made the commitment that he wouldn't be without a loved one by his side twenty-four hours a day. So we worked out a schedule between you, my husband, and me. I remember saying to you, "Not that we ever needed a nod from the universe for our commitment to friendship, but if you hadn't been there I think Rowan probably would've been a SIDS baby."

Kylee: There was a moment before he went to surgery when we were really scared about whether he was going to live. When they wheeled him off—that tiny baby in the middle of that big gurney—you knew that he was in the hands of the doctors and there was nothing more you could do. And that gave you comfort. But in that moment I realized there was nothing more that *I* could do, and I completely fell apart. And so we just switched roles.

Starr: I remember looking at you and thinking, *Wow, we really are two sides of the same heart.* Life was preparing us for this. And at that moment it was really clear: All those times we spent together as children and talking to each other on the phone when we were parted by thousands of miles—we were recommitting that we are best friends. We are soul mates.

Kylee: I don't think a day goes by that I don't look at that beautiful six-year-old with that scar on his chest and think how lucky we are.

RECORDED IN HARTFORD, CONNECTICUT, ON APRIL 14, 2007.

STARR COOKMAN *(left)*
AND KYLEE
MORELAND FENTON.

STEVEN WELLS, 57,

talks with his daughter,

JENNIFER WELLS, 27

Steven Wells: The last couple weeks before your due date, you decided to rotate inside your mother's stomach, so you had to be delivered through C-section, and it was kind of a touch-and-go delivery. You were very healthy, but your mother had to stay in the hospital for a week, so I brought you home by myself.

For the next week, I was Mr. Mom, and I was scared to death: *Oh my God—what am I going to do with this little tiny baby? I'm afraid I'm going to break it!*

I mean, I'm a blue-collar kind of guy—I worked in factories and construction. I was an ambulance driver and a medic in the air force, so I kind of knew a little bit, but it didn't help me when I brought home this little thing that I was just so afraid I was going to drop or squeeze or hurt. But you were pretty resilient.

All you did was eat, sleep, and poop, and that was pretty easy to take care of. But I was just in awe and amazement of what a beautiful little thing you were, and that you were a part of me. I thought, *Wow, the rest of my life is going to revolve around this child now. Everything has changed!* I knew things would never be the same again. I was a big teenager when you were conceived—twenty-nine years old and acting like I was nineteen—and then all of a sudden I had to grow up.

Shortly after you were born, things changed between your mother and me. I loved you more than myself, so I hung in there as long as I could. But by the time you were five years old, I knew I couldn't be married anymore.

When I finally told you, we took a walk and I was in tears trying to tell you that I wasn't going to be living at home anymore. And you put your arm around me and said, "Dad, it's okay. I'll get through it. I'm worried about you." I've never forgotten that. So I packed up my bags and I headed on down the road.

Jennifer Wells: I love that you stayed close. I was an only child, so you were my playmate. And even though you say you grew up, I'm glad you didn't grow up too much.

Steven: We both loved you so much that even though we quit taking care of each other, we tried to make sure that you had the upbringing you needed. And I raised you like the son I never had: I bought you dump trucks and baseball bats and mitts, and we'd dig in the sandbox with the pickup truck. I used to take you to the park and we'd throw the football around. We had my old air force duffel bag full of Frisbees, soccer balls, and footballs.

Jennifer: Yes, I loved that bag!

Steven: You were always kind of my buddy. Even though I'm your father and I tried to be an authority figure, I also tried to be the father to you that my father never was to me. When I was about ten years old, I was asking my dad to go out and play baseball with me, and he didn't want to. My mother started bugging him: "Come on, Bill. Go out and play with the boy." And I'll never forget hearing my dad say, "Jesus Christ, Kay! I'm the boy's father. If he wants to play with somebody, he can go up the street and play with one of the other kids!" I heard that and I just said, "Okay, well, I'm not going to be that kind of father."

His father did not play with him—he was a mean son of a gun. He disciplined them and whooped them and told them what to do, so my dad was the lawgiver, too. You have to discipline your children, but they look to their parents for all kinds of approval, and it's not enough to put food on the table and clothes on your back.

Jennifer: Well, I'm grateful that you decided to go a different route.

Steven: You asked me if I had any regrets. And you know, guilt sucks. There are things that I wish had happened differently or didn't happen, but everything that happened in my life is why I am here today—and why you're here. So no regrets. Some sadness, but you make it all worthwhile. I am honored to be your father, and I love you more than you will ever know.

RECORDED IN MACON, GEORGIA, ON MARCH 5, 2011.

Steven Wells passed away unexpectedly on September 19, 2011.

CHELDA SMITH, 24,

talks with her best friend,

GEORGIA SCOTT, 26

Chelda Smith: I remember growing up and picturing this fairy-tale life. The Huxtables had five kids, Brady Bunch had a whole *bunch* of kids—but I didn't have the family network that I wanted. So I just decided that my friends would have to make my picture come true.

When I was fifteen, I was on summer vacation in Atlanta from Boston, and I went to the local library just to find something to do—and I saw you. You're a talker, and we just really took off. While I was there for the summer, we hung out every day. I think we were both shopping for a good friend, and we became inseparable.

You told me about the HOPE Scholarship Program—how

if you graduate from a Georgia high school with a B or higher average, you can go to college for free. We were both going into the twelfth grade, so I convinced my parents to let me move down to Atlanta to go to school and get the scholarship. [*Laughter.*] And so I went to live with you.

Georgia Scott: You became a part of my family. We were unusually close, and we didn't include anybody else into our world—it didn't really matter who you were. It was Georgia and Chelda, Chelda and Georgia, and nobody else.

Chelda: We each had boyfriends, and if my boyfriend wanted to take me out—

Georgia: —he'd have to take both of us out. We went to the prom with one guy. He in the middle and one of us on either side. And we were perfectly fine with it! [*Laughs.*]

Chelda: Whatever I lacked, you had. And what you lacked, I had. We were two peas in a pod.

We chose the same college and we were roommates in this tiny, six-by-six dorm room. But even though we were roommates at your house, too, this was overkill.

Georgia: I don't think we've ever had this conversation before, but I had a boyfriend who needed a hundred percent of my attention. And you became a social butterfly in college and made other friends. Before it just used to be Georgia and Chelda, but now it was Georgia, Chelda, and a string of other people. And I don't think I really liked it. I left a year after, and that's sort of when we lost touch.

Chelda: We had two separate lives.

Georgia: I think I went maybe a year without speaking to you. And when we did speak, I felt like, *I might not feel like talking to you but I just have to make sure you're alive and kicking.*

Chelda: I always missed you, no matter what was going on, no matter how upset or angry or hurt I was. I thought, *We're not ever going to get back to normal. But if I know she's okay and I keep tabs on her, then I'll be fine.* So I started keeping a log of when I spoke to you.

There would be like three-, four-month increments between our conversations. And because our friendship had been so tight, I couldn't tell other people that we weren't friends anymore. People knew us as a couple, so when they would say, "How's Georgia?" "She's great!" [*Laughter.*]

After college, I went to New York to get my master's. I was working really hard. I was putting my little ducks in a row and then—*wham.*

Georgia: I remember you texted me, "I have something to tell you." And I kind of brushed you off. And then you texted me again and said, "I'm pregnant."

Chelda: I got pregnant my second year in grad school, and it was a secret. Nobody could know that I got pregnant out of wedlock. I was the one who was going to school and going to get the picket fence and all that, so it was a shock. But your reaction was exactly what I thought it'd be—

Georgia: I was there the following day.

Chelda: I had been by myself in New York, but you stayed the whole time and took care of me—cooked for me, cleaned for me—and didn't leave. I thought that was amazing. We'd argue, and you'd disappear for a day—and then come back to cook breakfast. [*Laughter.*]

Georgia: It was cool being there while you were pregnant, watching how your body changed, literally in front of my eyes. I saw the mood swings and the panic attacks and the back pain and all of it.

Chelda: You're not the most pro-baby person, but you were very positive.

We followed the books to the T, and I had an awesome pregnancy. Having my son was the best decision for me—and for our friendship.

Georgia: And I've learned that you are *the* positive factor in my life, and that no matter what the situation is, you're the one person that will show me that the glass is half full and not half empty. And I need that.

Chelda: In many ways, Georgia, you raised me. We had the memory of what our friendship was, and we fought for a long time to get it back. Because I always missed you, no matter how upset I was. And so now, even if we don't speak every day, I don't question whether our friendship is worth it. Now I fully understand what your role is in my life. You stepped up and were with me every day. So I just want to say, *Thank you.*

RECORDED IN ATLANTA, GEORGIA, ON NOVEMBER 12, 2009.

CHELDA SMITH *(left)*
AND GEORGIA SCOTT.

MYRA BROWN, 15,

talks with her mother,

BONNIE BROWN, 48,

who was born with an intellectual disability

Myra Brown: When you found out you were pregnant with me, what did you think?

Bonnie Brown: I was very happy, and I was also scared. I had never been pregnant before, and I had no idea how to care for a baby.

Myra: When Grandma was still alive, she offered to take me, but you said no. Did you ever feel like I was too much to handle?

Bonnie: No, never. You were just a wonderful thing to happen to me, and I really enjoyed you—and I still do now. I was going to give it all I got no matter what. I think because I'm different, it might seem hard for me, but I had this baby that I loved and that I carried for nine months. There was no way I was not going to take care of you, and I prayed to God that I would never have to give you up.

Myra: I didn't realize you were different when I was a kid. I just thought you did things differently. You actually had to tell me, because I wasn't figuring it out.

Bonnie: I said to you, "Myra, I know I'm not like your friends' mothers, but I'm doing the best I can and I love you." And you said, "It's okay, Mommy." And that made me feel so good.

Myra: I honestly didn't know, because you come off as someone who's basically normal, except for when you're walking down the street and say "Hi!" to everyone you see. You say "Hi!" to the cars as they drive by. [*Laughs.*]

And I remember when I was in third grade, you had to go in for my parent/teacher conference, and as a disclosure, I was like, "My mom's disabled." But the day after the interview, my teacher said that you seemed really intelligent. And it made me feel bad that I had said that.

Bonnie: Well, you were just giving her a heads-up, so no offense taken. You were just letting her know what she was dealing with.

Myra: So, what's the hardest thing you've had to overcome?

Bonnie: Being hurt by people.

Myra: There were times when we would go out and people would just blatantly stare at you. They would say things and be obnoxious, and I didn't like it. Of course, I would point out that they were being rude. I guess I'm protective.

Bonnie: People will do that—whether you have a disability or not. But I'm really thankful you understand me and you love me and you accept me.

Myra: You make it seem like I tolerate you, and it's not like that—I *love* you. Our situation is unique, but I'm happy because I'm with you. You try really hard and you're a good parent. But what I appreciate about you the most is how supportive you are.

I'm looking forward to college, because I'm going to meet tons of people and study really hard, but I'm also going to miss you.

Bonnie: I will miss you very much, but I want you to have your own life and succeed and do well. I wouldn't have it any other way.

RECORDED IN LANSDOWNE, PENNSYLVANIA, ON JANUARY 29, 2013.

Myra is in the gifted and talented program at her high school.

MARILYN GONZALEZ, 44,

talks with her daughter and fellow soldier,

JESSICA PEDRAZA, 21

Marilyn Gonzalez: We did our deployment together. But I was upset with you for a long time, because you had the opportunity to stay back.

Jessica Pedraza: I knew you were going to be upset, but I knew I'd rather be out there and be the first to know if something happened to you than sit and wait for somebody in dressing forms to come tell me.

For the first three months, we didn't see each other: I would be on a mission, come back, and then you would be on one. The first time we saw each other over there, I was literally five minutes from leaving on a mission. We shared a quick cry, and then I told you to relax and you told me to be safe.

Marilyn: It was hard to be "Sergeant Gonzalez" with you. We were both wearing the uniform, and we were both in the same unit, and every time I saw you I wanted to just go up and hug you. But I couldn't do it.

Jessica: When we were out there, we kept our mother/daughter relationship on the down low. But I couldn't look at you seriously and say, "Sergeant—" so I would sneak in a "Mom" once in a while. And whenever I came back from a mission, my bed would be completely made and you would always have a candy bar waiting for me. And you would make sure my boots and sneakers and shoes were all lined up.

Marilyn: My battle buddies would tease me all the time whenever they saw me making your bed.

Jessica: I was doing a radio check with you once, and I said, "Truck thirty-four, this is truck forty-seven, calling in for a radio check. How do you copy?" And you said, "It's a good copy." And I said, "Roger, I love you." And I heard you say it right back—you said it really, really quiet, but I caught it.

Marilyn: Whatever little messages I got from you kept me going. I never thought about how I was going to react if something happened to you—I just never wanted to think about that. So I thought, *She's going to go on her mission, and she's going to come back—and that's it.*

Jessica: You know, I didn't really have a close relationship with you before Iraq. I felt like I was the oddball of the five kids—I was the middle child, and I felt like I was just kind of on the side.

Marilyn: I felt that you were stronger and you didn't need me all the time. You were the one that always did what you said you were going to do. And you never really strayed from that, so it was easier for me to focus on the other ones. But it wasn't because I loved you any less.

Jessica: I really got to know you in Iraq. And I know that you were kind of upset that I gave up six college acceptances to do this with you. But being out there with you made me realize that you were there for me. It changed everything.

Marilyn: You're my daughter, and I love you. But you're also my battle buddy. And I could never tell you how much that means that you were willing to put your life on the line to be there with me.

Jessica: We have the mother/daughter bond *and* we have a soldier's bond. There's just nothing more you could ask for.

RECORDED IN ROCKLAND, MASSACHUSETTS, ON AUGUST 11, 2012.

This interview was a part of the StoryCorps Military Voices Initiative, which records stories of veterans, service members, and military families.

OTIS WADE, 73, talks to
BEATRICE PERRON DAHLEN, 24,
granddaughter of his friend
MANDRED HENRY,
on the eve of Mr. Henry's funeral

Otis Wade: I met Mandred in the first grade. We were born and raised in Hartford, Connecticut, but I moved to another part of the city and I didn't see him for a couple of years after that.

Then the next time I saw him we were going into junior high school. Mandred walked up to me and grabbed me by the shoulder and said, "You know what you are? You're my best friend in the whole wide world!" Mandred never had a brother, and I never had a brother, so we adopted one another. We understood one another. And we were always looking for one another and talking and sharing things.

He was a very outgoing young man, and even as a young kid he was very direct and forceful. He was my best friend but, *boy*, did we have a lot of arguments! Arguing was like entertainment between the two of us. Sometimes it got kind of serious—I mean, we were actually physically fighting—but we were like siblings and you couldn't separate one from the other.

Mandred and I would take our mothers out for Mother's Day together to a restaurant downtown in Hartford. I remember one day I was talking to his mother—a wonderful, vivacious little lady—and she said, "You two look after one another." And we have been ever since.

Beatrice Perron Dahlen: What about Papa makes you smile?

Otis: [*Laughs.*] A lot of things . . . That old gruffness of his . . .

Beatrice: I love thinking about how gruff he was because he acted so tough all the time, but he was just such a big teddy bear. And in the last couple of weeks, he was saying he was really worried about how you were going to take his death.

Otis: We had conversations with one another that we probably wouldn't have had with anybody else. We gave each other advice—counseling, if you will. We confided in one another and really believed in one another. I lost that presence of a person that had that confidence and belief in me and I had that confidence and belief in him.

I've had family members die: my mother, my father. But this is the first time I lost a friend. And the first one that I lost is my best friend in the whole wide world. So I have a deep feeling of loss . . . A greater part of me is gone.

RECORDED ON MARTHA'S VINEYARD, MASSACHUSETTS, ON MAY 11, 2007.

DENNIS DANIELS, 71,

talks with his longtime friend
LARRY ROLF, 66

Dennis Daniels: Sharon and I had our first date in October of 1990. Thanksgiving was coming up, and I asked her what she wanted to do. She said, "Well, let's go over to Larry's." I said, "Wait a minute. You want me to go over to your ex-husband's for Thanksgiving?"

Larry Rolf: Sharon and I had two kids together, and they always came over to my house at the holidays. And Sharon and my wife, Theresa, had become very good friends. So I didn't really have a problem when Sharon said that she was bringing somebody. You want to bring someone along, it's just another cup you add to the soup.

Dennis: So I said, "Well, I'll compromise. We'll go for an hour, and then we'll leave—"

Larry: But by about ten o'clock I thought, *Is this guy going to move in or what?*

Dennis: [*Laughs.*] We really hit it off. We had running in common, so we had something to talk about—and you're a great talker. And that's basically how it all started.

Sharon and I got married in June of 1991. We were wondering what to do for our honeymoon and I said, "I want to watch Larry finish his first marathon." And that's what we did.

Larry: I saw you and Sharon, and all of a sudden somebody I knew was there—I think I cried for joy. I mean, what better way to spend your honeymoon than seeing your ex-wife's husband come across the finish line? [*Laughter.*] I will always thank you for that.

Dennis: We have done a lot of things together over these twenty years, and I think Sharon was behind the relationship sticking. She was wonderful.

Larry: I think Sharon's last years with you were probably the happiest in her life, and I am so glad you got married. Sharon and I were only married for about six years—we were very good friends, but we should have just kept it that way. I was a complete horse's ass in the relationship. I was drinking, chasing. And Sharon was there taking care of the kids while I was out in bars. And how she made it—sometimes it just amazes me.

A couple of weeks before she died, we had a long conversation and I got to tell her how sorry I was, and it's helped me.

Dennis: Sharon was a wonderfully forgiving woman—I just admired her.

She was diagnosed in January 2007 with lung cancer, and she died January 2, 2009, two years later. You did the eulogy at Sharon's funeral, and you weren't sure you could get through it. I told you that I was behind you, and when you broke down I was there for you, as you've always been there for me.

Larry: Since Sharon passed, I try to call you daily.

Dennis: It's really nice to have somebody to talk to. You're more like a brother than a friend. You have been for a long time.

You were there for me when I was diagnosed with throat cancer and all through the radiation. And when we would go running together, you actually walked with me because I was so weak.

Larry: And now you walk with me because I can't keep up! [*Laughs.*]

Dennis: It's been almost two and a half years since Sharon's passing. When you lose somebody you love, it creates a hole in your soul that's hard to fill. But you have helped to fill that, and I appreciate that so very much.

Larry: You're my closest friend. And I expect that we're just going to continue on as long as we're on this side of the grass.

RECORDED IN BLOOMINGTON, MINNESOTA, ON APRIL 18, 2011.

LARRY ROLF *(left)*
AND DENNIS DANIELS.

WM. LYNN WEAVER, 57,

talks to his daughter,

KIMBERLY WEAVER, 38,

about his father, TED WEAVER,

who worked as a chauffeur and a janitor

Lynn Weaver: Growing up in Knoxville, Tennessee, we knew that there were certain things you just couldn't do—there were white-only water fountains and bathrooms—but you know, kids are kids. So we ran and played ball. I had an extremely happy childhood, I think, until high school, when the decision was made to integrate schools. And that's when childhood became not fun.

My brother and I were on the football team, and the first couple of years there were some teams that refused to play our team because we had black players. And the crowds were always verbally violent.

We had an away game in a little town outside of Knoxville. My brother was a linebacker, and I was the other linebacker. They ran a play and their number one player came running across the middle, and when he caught the ball my brother hit him high and I hit him low. He was injured. They put him on a stretcher, and the crowd went berserk. The crowd came onto the field—to my eyes it looked like maybe a thousand people, but probably it was only two hundred—and they were all shouting, "Kill the N-word! Kill the N-word!" And our whole team, black and white together, backed up against the fence. And I thought, *This is it. They are going to kill us.* And then an arm reached through the fence and grabbed my shoulder pads. I turned around and looked, and it was my father. He was very calm, and he said, "It's gonna be all right." I turned to my brother and I said, "Dad's here. We're gonna get out of this." He never missed a game.

Just then the state police came and escorted us to the bus. And when we got on the bus it dawned on me that my father was by himself—he was the only black man there. I knew the police wouldn't help him, and I figured if the crowd didn't get us, they would get him. And he just waved and the bus door closed and we took off. I was petrified.

When we got back to school, we went into the locker room and in walks my father. I never felt so happy in my life.

And like nothing had happened, he said, "You ready to go?" I said, "How did you get out of there?" And he said, "It was no problem." He never told us what happened. He never wanted us to worry about him; he just wanted us to know that if anything happened, he would be there to protect us.

I always tell you that your momma was the smartest person I've ever met, but I think my father ranks right up there as brilliant. He made me feel that I could do anything I wanted to do. When I was in high school, I was taking algebra, and one night I was sitting at the kitchen table trying to do my homework. I got frustrated and said, "I just can't figure this out." And my father said, "What's the problem? Let me look at it." I said, "Dad, they didn't have algebra in your day!" [*Laughter.*] And I went to bed.

At around four o'clock in the morning, he woke me up, and he sat me at the kitchen table and taught me algebra. What he had done was sit up all night and read the algebra book, and then he explained the problems to me so I could do them and understand them.

My father was everything to me. He was the greatest person I've ever known, the light of my life and the heart of my heart. Up until he died, I called him before every decision I made. He never told me what to do, but he would always listen and say, "Well, what do you want to do?"

So I live my life trying to be just half the man my father

was. And I would be a success if my children loved me half as much as I love my father.

RECORDED IN ATLANTA, GEORGIA, ON FEBRUARY 24, 2007.

Lynn Weaver is a surgeon.

THERESA THU-NGA NGUYEN, 47,
talks with her daughter, STEPHANIE
NGHIEM-AN NGUYEN, 24

Theresa Thu-Nga Nguyen: After the fall of Saigon in 1975, we tried to escape Vietnam—and the first eleven times we got caught. But finally, in 1978, Grandma was able to buy seats for us to leave on these very primitively built wooden boats. To this day, the journey is still in my mind, because going through a storm, the boat got beaten up and it broke apart—we were lucky to get to shore alive. We got to a little town in Thailand in the middle of the night, and we were taken into the refugee camp. About a year later, when I was seventeen, I was allowed to come to the United States.

So that's why your dad and I work so hard—and why we push our children so hard. You want your children to have a better life than you do. But many times when I look back on your upbringing, if I had to do it again, a couple of things I would have changed.

Stephanie Nghiem-An Nguyen: What would you do differently?

Theresa: I would be a little bit softer, a little more compromising. Remember some boy gave you a necklace?

Stephanie: And you made me go back to school the next day and give it back! [*Laughs.*]

Theresa: Okay, so things like that, I would go back and be a little bit more understanding. But I was taught from my mom: Do not accept presents from strangers, because if you accept presents from them, you have to repay them. It's a debt you have to carry to your grave, and that was engrained in my mind.

I am real gung-ho on keeping the tradition. I remember on Saturday and Sunday morning, Daddy taught you and your brother to read and write Vietnamese. I could tell that it wasn't your favorite time of the week, especially on the weekends. But I just wanted to preserve our culture and keep the family together.

Did you ever look and compare with your friends, if your mom is tougher than mine?

Stephanie: I don't even know where to start with that. [*Laughs.*] When you're twelve, and your whole world revolves around who went to whose birthday party, and who got to sleep over at whoever's house, it's not fun to say, "Oh no, I can't do that." But I think I learned a very strong sense of right and wrong, and that things don't get handed to you—you really have to work at it.

Theresa: Many of the things you mentioned, like sleepover at friends', I believe that if I didn't let you do it at all, you will forever be upset, and you might go out on a limb trying to do it on your own. So anything that you wanted, I gave you only once: sleepover, going out with friends, staying out late. I put a lot of rules and a lot of constraints on you and your brother growing up. But I'm very, very proud of you.

Stephanie: I'm glad that you're proud of me, because most of the time I feel like I'm a disappointment.

Theresa: No, you are not! You are not. [*Crying.*] I know many times I'm very proud of you, but I just never say it. Daddy gets on my case all the time: "You don't say it! You don't say it!" And I would tell him, "But she knows I feel it!" But I don't know if you know or not.

If I push you hard, it's good intention. It's from love. We have a purpose in life. And our purpose is to make sure that you don't have to go through the same thing that we go through. And I hope you understand that. I know a lot of times, in your mind, you guys always think of your daddy as the favorite parent . . .

Stephanie: Oh, no! That's terrible! I wouldn't say that.

Theresa: That's okay—somebody has to play the bad guy. [*Laughs.*] I don't mind one bit, as long as you turn out great.

Stephanie: I'm so appreciative of everything you've been through. And I want to be just like you. I only wish I could be half the mom that you are . . .

Theresa: Oh, you'll be better! I'm sure you'll be better. And hopefully, when you have your own children, you will learn from my mistakes. But I also hope that your upbringing with me wasn't *so* bad—when you have your children, maybe you might try to imitate a thing or two from me.

I hope that we get to understand each other a little better today. And when I go away from this life, I just want you to remember my love for you. That's all I want. I don't care for anything else.

RECORDED IN MORROW,
GEORGIA, ON MAY 1, 2010.

THERESA THU-NGA NGUYEN *(left)*
AND
STEPHANIE NGHIEM-AN NGUYEN.

GENNA ALPERIN, 12,

talks with her grandmother
MJ SEIDE, 58

Genna Alperin: How has your life been different than what you thought it was going to be?

MJ Seide: I thought that my life was probably not going to be worth living. There was this hole that I had all of my life, because I never thought I'd be able to walk along the beach and hold somebody's hand because I'm gay. I knew I was gay by the time I was four or five years old, and it was something that I certainly couldn't tell anybody. I didn't tell my friends; I didn't tell my parents. So I grew up thinking that I would never get married or have children.

But when I fell in love with Mamommy, I knew that she was my soul mate. I'd never felt that way about anyone before. After she had gotten her divorce from Grandpa Jim, she was very up front with her children—your mom and Uncle Justin—and told them that she was in love with a woman. That was the first time that anyone was open—or even proud—to say that they loved me. That just made me the happiest I'd ever been in my life.

When I finally came out to my family in 1981, which is not that long ago, my brother disowned me. He wouldn't let me be with my ten-year-old niece because he was so educated about what being gay is. But when I got to know your mom, she couldn't be closer to me if she was my own daughter. When I saw how happy she was that Mamommy was happy, I knew that I had hit paradise, because I now have a family that I can wrap my arms around. Then, once your mom got married and Uncle Justin got married and they both started trying to have children, I realized, *Wow—I really could have the American dream of having a family and grandchildren someday!*

From the very day that I found out that your mommy was pregnant, I would call her and say, "Okay, let me talk to the baby." And she would put the phone to her belly and I would just chat with you. I would sing you every kind of song— "Rock-a-Bye" and so forth. And she would just sit there and read or do something else while she kept the phone on her belly. And so I talked to you every single day.

You were born at 1:19 a.m., and when I got to the hospital, I went directly to the nursery. I walked into that room and over to your bassinet, and you were just screaming at the top of your lungs. But as soon as I opened my mouth and said, "Hello, Genna," you immediately stopped crying and you tried to find me with your eyes. Your eyes were searching and your head was turning, trying to find that voice that you had been listening to. From the day you were born, you and I were kindred spirits, I think. I don't see how we could be any closer.

You know, this is the first time we've ever talked about the fact that I'm gay. You've never asked about me and Mamommy, and I guess what I want to ask you is, does it embarrass you to have a gay grandma?

Genna: No . . . 'cause what matters is my relationship with you. You're one of my favorite grandmas, and I love you a lot. [*Crying.*] You do a lot of things with me, like ride roller coasters and play poker. And I don't know what life would be like without you here . . .

MJ: I always tell you how much I love you, but I don't know that you can really understand the depth of it. You're someone that I never thought would be in my life. And you are such a part of me.

RECORDED IN NORFOLK, VIRGINIA, ON OCTOBER 28, 2009.

BARBARA HANDELSMAN, 80,

talks to her grandson

AARON HANDELSMAN, 20

Barbara Handelsman: When I was really little, I thought my younger sister had all the power, because she was pudgy and cute, where I was all elbows and knees—there was nothing pretty about me at all. I was so shy; I had no idea how to be the popular kid at a party. I didn't have any way of integrating myself with other children, and I felt incompetent when it came to trying to be an A-plus *anything* with adults—except for my aunt Virginia, my mother's oldest sister.

I have riveted in my memory bank still: my aunt coming into the house and I've just conquered a book I was reading or a picture I had drawn, and her saying, "Oh, Barbs!" She was so impressed that her tears would practically run. And then tears would run down *my* face because she was so impressed.

Whatever it was I had been up to, she thought it was marvelous. This was when I was nine and a half and skinny as a rail—and she made me feel like I was all right, whatever I was.

And then I discovered the outdoors, and something inside of me went on like a light. I loved everything about it. I loved that I could look straight up at the sky and watch the clouds change. And at night watch the sun go down and the moon come up. I could go and sit on a hill at the nearest park and do nothing in particular—just be there.

Aaron Handelsman: I never heard you talk about feeling so isolated when you were younger. I didn't realize that you felt that way. I can identify—but I've always had *you.* I guess that's why I hold you so highly in my life.

Do you remember when you'd moved to Ypsilanti, and we had those inflatable kayaks that we took on the Huron River? I think I was about sixteen years old and I couldn't wait to go and brag to my friends about how I had such a cool, badass grandmother who was kayaking down a river with me. [*Laughter.*] I think you were seventy-six or seventy-seven at the time.

Barbara: We have a very positive effect on each other.

Aaron: I agree. I've been meaning to sit down with you and ask you questions for a long time, and this seems like a good opportunity. So, what is a really fulfilling moment for you?

Barbara: Well, it's funny you should ask, because they are the kinds of things that happen on our trips. When we're in a river, for heaven's sake, that isn't anything especially remarkable. But my experience with you is that I'm always perfectly free to be me.

I have lots of people in my family who think I'm okay, but they really wished I'd change my engine here and turn that screw and fix it so it doesn't do this or it does do that. There's just something about me that they would rather fix. But not you, Aaron. I can be any way I want to be, and it's perfectly all right with you.

Aaron: And I feel the same. We're both pretty quirky—and we have complementary quirks—so it all kind of works out. I think we bring out the best in each other.

Barbara: Well, Aaron, I have some advice. And my advice is: Be yourself. Don't let any adult ever convince you that you should be somebody else, or try to give a cheerful "Ho! Ho! Ho!" personality if that's not who you are. Just be who you are. That's the single thing.

Aaron: We've had a lot of heart-to-hearts, but I don't know if I've ever just told you how much I feel like you've introduced me to a lot of the things that make me who I am:

the love for the outdoors, and just the freedom to be myself and to not worry about saying or doing something others may consider to be foolish. You're an incredible person and one of the most inspirational and admirable people in my life.

RECORDED IN ANN ARBOR, MICHIGAN, ON SEPTEMBER 4, 2008.

Barbara Handelsman passed away on May 17, 2010.

FRANK W. LILLEY, 59,

talks with his stepfather,

DAVID W. PLANT, 80

In 2010, David was diagnosed with terminal cancer.

Frank Lilley: You first met me when I was about nine or ten years old, when you married my mother. I'm just wondering what your impressions were of me at the time.

David Plant: You were an athletic, good-looking, nice guy, but you were in the unhappy situation of having a broken family.

Frank: My parents were divorced in about 1956. Divorce was a lot less common at that time than it is now, and so when I was a kid, I felt like an outsider. I had to explain all the time why I had two sets of parents. I didn't have a lot of people to look up to—or a lot of friends, really.

My family was having a lot of trouble, but I remember

you and my mother as a haven away from the drinking and the fighting. I think, honestly, that gave me a stability that I've carried with me for all my life. You very rapidly became someone I looked up to. You set the example.

David: I didn't realize at the time that you felt that way. I might have done more in helping you get through adolescence if I'd known. But I was a little apprehensive about getting too close to someone whose father was still around.

I think a watershed in our relationship was the time when you were living with us. I didn't tolerate pot smoking in the apartment, and I said it's either no pot smoking or you're out. And so, regrettably, it created an enormous chasm in our relationship.

Frank: That's something I've always wanted to discuss with you, because I don't think we've ever reconciled it. There's been a perception in this family that you threw me out of the house. I was about sixteen or seventeen, and I certainly was pot smoking, but I was also just having a very hard time living with my mother. You put that on top of the turmoil that was going on—the Vietnam War, the protests, the civil rights movement—and it was a very disturbing time for me.

So when you came to me and said, "You either follow the rules of this house or you have to leave," I said, "I just think I'll move on." So you didn't throw me out. But I think it was the biggest mistake of my life when I left, because it was so hard for me to go from having opportunities to being a high school dropout. I felt a lot of guilt about *that*, but I always respected you.

David: Wow . . . Thank you.

Frank: I don't have a lot of regrets, but I do regret that we have not talked like this sooner.

David: We coast around and talk about the weather or something, but we never get down to anything serious. I want to have more conversations like this, too. We're now saying things that we should have said a hundred years ago.

Frank: You know, I was thinking the other day of how long I've looked up to you, and I realized that's what I'm doing right now, again. I'm watching and I'm trying to learn. *How are you handling all this?*

David: I don't fear death. Dying is the end of life, and this is a journey toward that end. But it's certainly rewarding—and exciting sometimes. Look at this opportunity to talk with you, for example—it's just incredible. So I'm finding that this end-of-life journey I'm on isn't all bad.

Frank: What would you like to see happen after you pass?

David: I would just like people to believe that humility, listening, forgiving, and trying to understand the other person are important. And if people can begin to believe that, maybe there will be a little more peace and calm.

Frank: You're the glue that keeps this family together. We all love you and admire you. And now somebody I've learned to love and call a father is going to be gone.

David: I think in a year from now, it's quite possible that I won't be here. But the memory and the love will live on.

RECORDED IN NEW LONDON, NEW HAMPSHIRE, ON MARCH 16, 2012.

David Plant passed away on September 26, 2012.

This interview was a part of the StoryCorps Legacy Initiative.

DAVE SHEA, 55,

talks to his best friend,

ALICE DOYLE, 59

Dave Shea: I told my father that I was coming home to help him remodel his house after my mother died. I was only going to stay a few months, but then I met people in Butte and fell in love with the place. So I decided to stay.

My dad got real cranky after he retired, and he loved his crankiness. One of the things I noticed early on was that he had all these small coffee cans lined up in the garage, and I'd say to him, "Dad, wouldn't it be cheaper to buy larger cans of coffee and have less garbage?"

And he'd say, "Oh, leave me alone! It's my house! I do what I want." And so they kept stacking up in the garage.

And several months after I had moved home, he said to me, "Would you go buy a bag of sand, some rolls of colored aluminum foil, and as many silk flowers as you can get? Don't ask me—just go do it for me, would you, please?" So I said, "Sure, no problem." And I got all the stuff he'd asked me to get.

The day after, I was having breakfast, and he came out wearing bib overalls and a snap-brim cap. And he said to me, "Would you mind helping me with the graves today?"

I thought it was my mom's grave and my grandparents' grave, and I thought I'd enjoy going out there with him. But when we get out to the garage, he's got shovels and rakes and clippers and a trunk full of bouquets in coffee cans. I said, "What are we doing?" He goes, "We're doing the graves. Just be quiet and let's go."

So we got in the car and we drove to the cemetery. En route, he told me how when they were kids he lived with his mother, who was a miner's widow, his two maiden aunts, and his two sisters in a foursquare on Boardman Street. They would get on the streetcar on top of Montana, and take it to the end of the line. And then, all dressed in black and wearing their rosary beads, carrying their tools and their lunches and their flowers, they'd walk to the cemetery. They'd spend the day doing the graves, saying a rosary at each grave, and then at sundown they would get on the last car that went up the hill and go home.

And I just thought, *Wow. I've known you all my life. I've never heard this story.* We did my grandmother's grave and my mother's. And then we got back in the car and started driving around the cemetery, looking for these other graves. I said, "Who are these people?" My dad said, "These are the people that helped me through my life. They don't have any relatives, and they don't have any survivors, and every year I do their graves."

We stopped at a grave, and it said "Mr. and Mrs. Torpy." And I said, "Who are they? I've never heard of them." He said, "We were poor, and we didn't have anything. And when I needed to learn how to drive a car, Mr. Torpy taught me. And when I had to have a car to go on a date or something, Mr. Torpy would loan me his Buick."

So that's pretty much how the day went. My dad never spoke about his past, and we never talked about where he came from. But that day, through the process of paying tribute to the people that helped him out, I heard my dad's whole life history.

Ten years later, the day before Father's Day, my dad died.

One day, I was at the airport—it's right adjacent to the cemetery. Looking out, there's maybe forty acres of plastic flowers. And this one guy said, "My God, isn't that tacky?" I just looked at him, and I might have agreed with him in another life, but all of a sudden I realized: *Well, no. It's not tacky. It's beautiful.*

RECORDED IN BUTTE, MONTANA, ON JULY 7, 2007.

Acknowledgments

This is a book about gratitude, and there's a lot to go around.

Soup to nuts this book was skillfully and gracefully conceived, edited, and shepherded to completion by Lizzie Jacobs. Enormous gratitude also to Maya Millett and Makeba Seargeant of our print department for their hard work and commitment to excellence. Additional thanks to Ryan Salim, Wendy Sekimura, Lucas Adams, and Kelly Shetron. Gratitude to researcher Eve Claxton and fact-checkers Laura Griffin and James Thilman, as well as to the Audio Transcription Center and Jennifer Kotter. For support and advice throughout, profound gratitude to Donna Galeno and Kathrina Proscia.

We feel so fortunate to have a home at the Penguin Press,

the best publisher in the business. Thanks to our extraordinarily talented and dedicated editor, Lindsay Whalen, as well as to Ann Godoff, Scott Moyers, Yamil Anglada, Tracy Locke, and Ben Platt. Thanks always to our agent, David Black, who has our back all day, every day.

Gratitude to our friends and family at NPR, the Library of Congress, and the hundreds of other national and local partners we work with across the country each year. Special thanks to our steadfast group of funders and donors, including Pat Harrison and the Corporation for Public Broadcasting, and our board of directors led by Gara LaMarche.

Profound thanks to those who have worked at StoryCorps over the past decade. This book is for you.

And thanks to the one hundred thousand participants and millions of listeners, watchers, readers, and believers who have given StoryCorps life. This is only the beginning.

STORYCORPS TIMELINE

October 2003   StoryCorps opens in New York's Grand Central Terminal.

May 2005   StoryCorps launches two MobileBooths—traveling recording studios housed in Airstream trailers—which begin traveling across the nation.

May 2005   StoryCorps' weekly Friday broadcasts debut on NPR's *Morning Edition*.

July 2005   StoryCorps launches its first special initiative—the September 11th Initiative—to remember the lives lost on 9/11, in partnership with the September 11 Memorial & Museum at the World Trade Center.

July 2006   StoryCorps launches the Memory Loss Initiative, with a focus on families affected by Alzheimer's.

February 2007   StoryCorps launches the Griot Initiative to collect the stories of African American families across the nation, in partnership with The Smithsonian Museum of African American History and Culture.

November 2007   The first StoryCorps book, *Listening Is an Act of Love*, is released by The Penguin Press and becomes a *New York Times* bestseller.

November 2008   StoryCorps launches the first annual National Day of Listening on the day after Thanksgiving to encourage people to record do-it-yourself interviews with loved ones.

September 2009   StoryCorps launches the Historias Initiative to celebrate Latino stories across the country.

July 2010   StoryCorps launches the Legacy Initiative to provide people with serious illnesses and their families the opportunity to record, preserve, and share their stories.

August 2010   StoryCorps' animated shorts premiere on public television and receive millions of views online.

September 2011   StoryCorps rolls out its education program for at-risk youth, StoryCorpsU, in New York City, Washington, D.C., and St. Louis.

December 2012   StoryCorps launches its Military Voices Initiative, honoring the stories of active-duty service members, veterans, and family members of post-9/11 conflicts.

October 2013   StoryCorps records its fifty thousandth interview and celebrates its tenth anniversary.

FAVORITE STORYCORPS QUESTIONS

- What was the happiest moment of your life? The saddest?

- Who was the most important person in your life? Can you tell me about him or her?

- Who has been the biggest influence on your life? What lessons did that person teach you?

- Who has been the kindest to you in your life?

- What are the most important lessons you've learned in life?

- What are you proudest of in your life?

- Are there any words of wisdom you'd like to pass along to me?

- How has your life been different than what you'd imagined?

- How would you like to be remembered?

- Do you have any regrets?

- What does your future hold?

- Is there anything that you've never told me but want to tell me now?

- Is there something about me that you've always wanted to know but have never asked?

CONTINUE THE CONVERSATION

Visit www.storycorps.org to

- support StoryCorps

- learn how to interview someone important to you

- listen to more stories and share them with others

- view our animated shorts

- subscribe to our podcast

- find out where our booths are located and how to bring StoryCorps to your community

- check out StoryCorpsU, our college readiness curriculum, as well as other resources for educators

- read about (and participate in!) the National Day of Listening

One hundred percent of the royalties from this book will be donated to StoryCorps, a not-for-profit organization.

Lead funding for StoryCorps comes from the Corporation for Public Broadcasting.

Major funders include the Atlantic Philanthropies, the Boeing Company, Cancer Treatment Centers of America, the Ford Foundation, the Marc Haas Foundation, the Kaplen Foundation, the John D. and Catherine T. MacArthur Foundation, and Joe and Carol Reich.

Additional funders include Allstate Insurance Company, the BayTree Fund, Bloomberg Philanthropies, the Joyce Foundation, the National Endowment for the Arts, the New York City Department of Cultural Affairs, the Open Society Foundations, and the Tides Foundation.

Legal services are generously donated by Latham & Watkins and Holland & Knight.

For a complete and current list of all of our supporters, please visit our Web site: www.storycorps.org.

National partners include American Folklife Center, Smithsonian National Museum of African American History and Culture, National September 11 Memorial & Museum, National Public Radio, PBS, and POV.

AVAILABLE FROM PENGUIN

All There Is
Love Stories from StoryCorps

In *All There Is*, StoryCorps founder Dave Isay shares stories from the revolutionary oral history project, revealing the many remarkable journeys that relationships can take. This powerful collection enriches our understanding of love and the resilience of the human spirit.

ISBN 978-0-14-312302-6

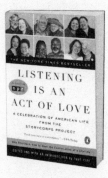

Listening Is an Act of Love
A Celebration of American Life from the StoryCorps Project

The voices here connect us to real people and their lives—to their experiences of profound joy, sadness, courage, and despair. The StoryCorps project represents a wondrous celebration of our shared humanity, capturing for posterity the stories that define us and bind us together.

ISBN 978-0-14-311434-5

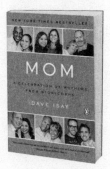

Mom
A Celebration of Mothers from StoryCorps

With this vital contribution to the American storybook, StoryCorps has created a tribute to mothers that honors the wealth of our national experience. An appreciation of the wisdom and generosity passed between mothers and children, *Mom* offers powerful lessons in the meaning of family and the expansiveness of the human heart.

ISBN 978-0-14-311880-0

PENGUIN
BOOKS